D0571275

NORTHUMBERLAND COUNTY LIBRARY

You should return this book on or before the last date stamped below unless an extension of the loan period is granted.

Application for renewal may be made by letter or telephone.

Fines at the approved rate will be charged when a book is overdue.

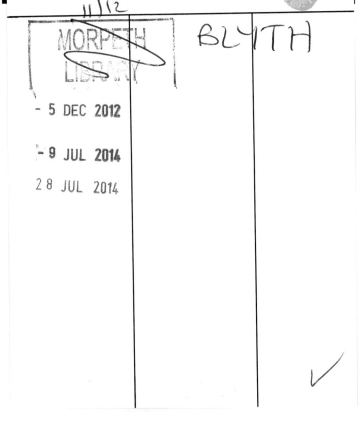

ANCESTORS IN THE ATTIC

MAKING FAMILY MEMORABILIA INTO HISTORY

KAREN FOY

The History Press

For Jeff – Love Always. With thanks for your support, encouragement and honest opinions during my latest venture. This one's for you!

Front cover images: Lightbulb in attic (Bryce Kroll/ iStockphoto); all other images courtesy of Karen Foy and Stewart Coxon.

First published 2012

The History Press
The Mill, Brimscombe Port
Stroud, Gloucestershire, GL5 2QG
www.thehistorypress.co.uk

British Library Cataloguing in Publication Data.
A catalogue record for this book is available from the British Library.

ISBN 978 0 7524 6428 2

Typesetting and origination by The History Press
Printed in Great Britain
Manufacturing managed by Jellyfish Print Solutions Ltd

CONTENTS

ACKNOWLEDGEMENTS

Thank you to The History Press for giving me the opportunity to write another book. I have enjoyed the research as much as the writing. Thank you to Stewart Coxon for providing some excellent images for illustration and for those kindly supplied by The Advertising Archives and Mulready Philatelics.

Writing and research can be a time-consuming and intensive profession requiring dedication to overcome regular writerly hurdles. I've often found that it wouldn't be possible without the support and encouragement of family and friends, so thanks to you all, and especially to my husband Jeff for his regular 'words of wisdom', my auntie Margaret Turner and my mother-in-law Marjorie Martin for 'spurring me on', and Enid Jones, unofficial 'agent' and friend, for her unwavering interest in my work.

INTRODUCTION

For the majority of family historians, once you have dipped your toe in the water of this fascinating pastime it is very hard to stop researching. The compulsion to find out more takes over and then you're well and truly addicted to this genealogical world.

Perhaps you recognise the scenario: you have endless lists of names, dates and places stored in files or on your dedicated computer program along with a whole host of neatly accumulated birth, marriage and death certificates relating to the most significant members of your ancestry. Transcripts of parish records threaten to spill from your folders and you've spent many enjoyable hours investigating family occupations that have now become long-forgotten trades.

Although your tree has branched out to encompass distant cousins, the quest for new names becomes more difficult the further back you go. Perhaps you simply feel that you want to concentrate more on those ancestors who are closer to you. If you've read my previous book, *Family History for Beginners* (The History Press) you may have gone down the route of preserving your findings in a variety of ways to share with your family, but like all historians, you are eager to go that one step further in finding out about your ancestors' lives. For me, this next stage is to look more closely at the physical evidence they left behind and build a bigger picture of life in a particular period by discovering what people wore, the items they used to decorate their homes, ephemera collected from memorable events, as well as letters, photographs and journals that document an individual's thoughts, feelings and hopes for the future.

It is time to step inside our ancestors' shoes in an attempt to learn more. At the beginning of any genealogical journey I always advise new starters to dig out all their family memorabilia to see what clues they may hold to their heritage, but as the pursuit of names and dates takes over, these items often get pushed aside as you become absorbed in the research. Now, along with the mass of information you have already collected, it is time to re-examine those items and reveal their secrets.

This quest for knowledge is all about looking at the evidence from a different angle. A photograph that initially may have meant nothing to you could now hold the key to a family puzzle; items in the background of the image could still exist and be residing in a relative's cupboards. An indenture or mortgage document relating to a property that you thought had no connection to your forebears could, in fact, have been the childhood home of one particular branch of your tree. Sporting trophies, clothing, accessories and childhood games may now be attributed to an individual, and a diary entry of a trip abroad relating to what at first seemed like a bunch of strangers could spark recognition.

You have now taken on the role of your family's 'lost and found' department and your mission is to find out more about the items that have stood the test of time but may be living in your attic or those of other family members.

This task also has a dual purpose. Perhaps you may not have been fortunate enough to have inherited many items from your ancestors. If that is the case, the wealth of antiques, collectables and ephemera available today from fairs, car-boot sales, specialist auctions and internet websites will allow you to build your own dedicated archive. Seek out an example of the type of newspaper an ancestor of yours is likely to have read in 1880 and discover what was happening in the world at that time. Perhaps family photos show a female ancestor who was never seen without her elaborate tortoiseshell hair accessories or elegant shoe buckles; why not track down some similar period examples to add to your archive, enabling future generations to touch and examine the fashion items of the past?

Uncover the treasures that were once part of everyday life and discover that each and every one has a story to tell. Combine your tried and tested research skills with the physical evidence before you. Take a second look at those 'ancestors in the attic' and you may be surprised at what details can be brought to light. Learn more about the history that surrounds some of these objects with help from the various in-depth 'Step Back in Time' sections in this book and discover their significance in your fore-bears' lives. A wider knowledge leads to a better understanding of events or the reasons behind an individual's actions.

Enjoy building that bigger picture and you'll soon begin to realise that investigating your ancestry can turn into a long-term project where the possibilities are endless and only limited by the boundaries you set.

CHAPTER BREAKDOWN

1. Putting Pen to Paper

Diary keeping, its aim and purpose. Famous diarists. How thematic examples, such as war diaries, personal accounts of everyday life and occupational diaries, can aid the family or local historian. Almanacs, their history and their importance to farming communities.

How to use diaries to build a picture of what life was like during different periods. How to track down themed examples to aid research. Investigation and preservation techniques.

2. Travel and Transport

Investigating travel-related ephemera. Understanding travel journals, their mention of varying types of transport, from sailing barques to steam trains, and the locations visited during Grand Tours. Discovering the reasons why people travelled. Britain's first travel agent, Thomas Cook, his organisation of day trips and global excursions. The Temperance movement, understanding its purpose and the ephemera and propaganda produced. The history and traditions of British seaside holidays and the related memorabilia produced.

3. A Stamp of Approval
Understanding the history of the postal and stamp system. Examining different letter, envelope and postal formats. Victorian correspondence, essential etiquette.

4. Reading Between the Lines
War-related ephemera. Enhancing your military investigations with medals, badges, buckles, tags and war propaganda posters. Embroidered postcards produced, especially during the war years. Military memorabilia and media coverage.

5. Regulations and Restrictions
Home front memorabilia. Understanding this period in history. Investigating why each item was issued and the restrictions they would impose upon our ancestors' lives. The role and related ephemera of the Home Guard, ARP Wardens and Women's Land Army.

6. Setting the Scene
Understanding the history of map-making. Topographical and local-interest ephemera. Maps, walkers' guides, directories, street plans, leaflets and tourist pamphlets and posters. Understanding more about the area and places of note in the locality where our ancestors lived or the destinations to which they travelled.

7. Customers and Commerce: Letterheads, Bills and Receipts
Indentures and apprenticeships: did your ancestor leave evidence of a trade? Business stationery, including letterheads, ledgers and receipts. Trade journals and occupational memorabilia. Prosperity or poverty: what clues can this type of ephemera provide? Investments: stocks and share certificates, mortgages and legal documents. Using legal documents to further your research to discover names, addresses, specific locations, trading names, land and property ownership.

8. Artistic Advertising
Business promotion, the ephemera that binds customers and commerce. Trade cards, advertising and promotional packaging. Uncovering your ancestors' likes and dislikes, shopping and eating habits.

9. Photography
The development of photography. Recognising photographic procedures. Dating dilemmas and identification problems: how to close the net. Photo storage and preservation.

10. Events, Entertainment and Opinions

How greetings cards can confirm family relationships and ages. Popular period entertainment. How newspaper cuttings and reviews, theatre programmes and show-business publications of the day can enlighten us about the music, theatre, books, famous personalities and events that our ancestors enjoyed. Suffragettes; following our ancestors' political beliefs.

11. A Lasting Reminder

Using newspapers to widen your genealogical research and understanding of life during a particular period. The history behind publications such as *The Illustrated London News*, *The Sphere*, *The Graphic* and *Punch*. Where to find these publications; the importance of this type of resource and how to preserve it.

12. Changing Fashions

Iconic clothing and fashions through the decades from the Victorian era to the 1920s, continuing to the Second World War, and their ability to help you to date your photographs. Mourning robes and their meaning. The Victorian wedding dress; choosing the right colour fabric. The christening gown; the importance of lasting legacies. The preservation and storage of fabrics.

13. Decorative Essentials: Accessories, Jewellery and Watches

Decorative accessories that were deemed important enough to our ancestors to bequeath to future generations. Hair combs and the styles they embellished. Parasols and umbrellas. Buttons. Beaded bags and how to date your examples. Lockets and love tokens. Perfumes, the decorative containers used to house them and their significance to our forebears. Masculine embellishments; timepiece identification, walking canes and decorative cufflinks and pins.

14. Habits and Hobbies

Smoking and smoking collectables. Sewing boxes, lace-making, embroideries and tapestries, quilting and patchwork; the history behind them and the clues they can give us.

15. Sporting Memorabilia

Medals and trophies awarded at sporting events may hold the key to your ancestors' past. Sporting almanacs. Cigarette cards. How to build a sporting archive.

16. Kings of the Road

The popularity of the motor car from the end of the nineteenth century. Was your ancestor a keen motorist? Discovering why motoring manuals, price guides and publications, as well as advertising and apparel, could help you build a bigger picture of their passion.

17. Playtime and Pastimes

Childhood toys can reveal a great deal about our ancestors' youth. Consider what their games can tell us about their personalities and upbringings. Which games were popular during which era? Determine how education and religion featured in some toy themes.

18. Household Essentials

Learn how the simplest of household objects can throw light on the daily lives of our ancestors. Customs and traditions within the home and the history behind them.

19. Checklist

ONE

PUTTING PEN TO PAPER

Writing is an exploration. You start from nothing and learn as you go.
E.L. Doctorow

Rifling through the personal possessions of deceased family members can often seem like prying, but it is surprising how many long-forgotten secrets you can discover, or which unanswered questions you can solve. Any number of items could have been handed down within a family or bequeathed as a lasting legacy, it is just that some pieces of memorabilia, ephemera and what are now today's collectables, tell greater stories than others.

If you're lucky enough to unearth a personal diary or journal then you really have struck gold. Used to record a person's innermost thoughts and feelings, as well as to chart the year's events and daily activities, this is one of the few opportunities that you'll have to really get inside your ancestor's mind.

HISTORY IN THE MAKING

From great historical writers such as Samuel Pepys and Dr Johnson to the wild and imaginative jottings of the fictional Adrian Mole, keeping a diary has been a popular pastime for thousands of people throughout the centuries. Samuel Pepys, Britain's most famous diarist, was born in 1633 and went on to become an MP and naval administrator while keeping a detailed private journal from 1660 to 1669. His jottings provide witness accounts of fascinating events during this decade, such as the Great Fire of London and the effects of the plague, but also offer personal details that we could never hope to find in a history book.

Diary keeping became increasingly popular from the seventeenth century onwards with many factors contributing to an interest in this pursuit of recording memories. Advances in the education system saw a growth in literacy among the population, and those with religious beliefs began questioning their faith. Others chronicled the births, marriages and deaths of family members, describing these events in detail for future generations. This was an era when paper production became cheaper and more

Thoughts and feelings can be found written in the hand of an individual in personal diaries, providing priceless information that you could not hope to find elsewhere.

affordable for personal use, allowing the diary to become a sanctuary for the author's thoughts and observations.

There is nothing quite like the excitement of discovering a diary, or any form of personal correspondence that has been lovingly stored away for decades in an old chocolate or cigar box that obviously meant so much to the original owner that they felt compelled to keep it. Regularly disposed of as just the personal trappings of the deceased, any such writing that avoids being tossed out with the rubbish or lies hidden for years only to be discovered by an enthusiastic benefactor can form part of a fascinating collection – priceless to a descendant – but can also provide an intriguing glimpse into a particular period of time, which can aid your own investigations.

THE ORGANISED APPROACH

The following tips can be applied to your study of any type of correspondence, not only diaries:
* Always read the document through once to get a general idea of what it contains and then, with a critical approach, take a closer look at what you've got.
* Note down all the facts, dates and addresses, along with any assumptions that you may have made.

* Add descriptive information about the interior of the writer's home, the car they drove or even the clothing they were wearing at the time.
* Log any questions that need answering and future avenues of research that you can pursue.
* Keep all your notes, even when you've found the answers, as they are always helpful to refer to at a later date and may inspire another train of thought for you to follow.

From the rich to the poor, the agricultural labourer to the lord of the manor, a diary and personal reminiscence can transport you back in time.

Ask yourself:
* Is the diary themed, for example, an occupational aid used to jot down the notes of a lawyer or doctor. Is it a war diary recollecting the feelings of someone involved in a conflict, or the recorded travel exploits of the family adventurer (see Chapter 2)?
* Was the diary created solely to record a specific event or period? Why was this important to the writer?
* What does it tell you about everyday life at the time?
* What kind of relationship did the writer have with their family? Did they have a happy marriage, or was their diary keeping a means of escape from a trapped or unhappy relationship?
* What was happening in the world at the time? Did the writer mention world events and, if so, what was their reaction to them?
* Did the writer have aspirations, ambitions or hopes for the future and were they ever fulfilled?
* Look for additions and inclusions: memorable items that the user thought important enough to paste between the pages. These could include sketches, verses, sentiments, tickets, postcards and other paper ephemera. Take a closer look, what can they tell you?

Top Tip   Where diaries are written in a plain notebook and only the day and month dates are recorded, use an online calendar calculator such as *http://easycalculation.com/date-day/dates.php* to try and pinpoint the year in which it was written. N.B. The same technique can be used on other letters and documents where the specific year has not been noted. Recorded events within the document may also help to provide a time frame.

PRESERVING THE PAST

Where possible make a copy of the document: this will save on wear and tear during your research. Use a photocopier with an adjustable panel that allows the copying of larger diaries to ensure that the spine is not bent, broken or creased. Store copies away from the originals so that if one becomes lost or damaged you will always have the other.

Keep items in as near perfect condition as possible by storing in a cool, dry place out of direct sunlight. Wrap in archival paper, which is acid and lignum free to help with long-term preservation, and if the item is extremely delicate consider wearing cotton gloves while handling.

Paper ephemera can rip easily and after years of being folded in a certain way, may become fragile along fold lines. Contemplate transcribing entries that are difficult to read onto your computer, to help make future reference easier.

Never write notes – even in pencil – on your original copy and don't cut or remove any loose pieces, always keep everything original together.

Find Out More

A diary does not have to have belonged to a member of your ancestry to add background information or understanding of a particular period to your family tree. There are literally thousands of manuscripts, letters and documents up for sale on websites like *www.ebay.co.uk*. It is just a matter of searching for items and subjects that interest you. Whittling down your search with phrases such as 'travel', 'military', 'WW2' or 'naval' can help you pinpoint the gems out there.

If you're inspired by military memorabilia, look out for war diaries, regimental descriptions, letters from remote outposts or descriptive love notes written from the trenches.

Is it a topographical area that interests you? Do you want to find out more about the town or village where your ancestors grew up? Target your searches to that region.

Is there a specific occupation that you would like to find out more about? Unusual trades with illustrated letterheads can shed light on business dealings and prices charged for services offered. From the simple transactions of a rural grocer to the commerce of traders in exotic locations, documents still exist with vivid explanations of everyday life in another era.

Are you drawn towards social history, with a fascination for life in a particular century, the clothes worn and the daily routines carried out? Observations have been penned on every subject, it is just a matter of seeking them out.

Book fairs, attic sales and antique fairs are great places to begin your quest. Don't forget to rummage through boxes of junk at car-boot sales for those long-forgotten treasures and search the sites of specialist ephemera dealers to see what kind of items are on offer. Remember that each example is unique, so consider that factor when setting yourself a budget.

Some of the most absorbing diaries have been transcribed and are now readable online.

Step back in time and follow the everyday exploits of Samuel Pepys at *www.pepys-diary.com*. Awash with famous names of the day, it also gives us a window into life in seventeenth-century London.

If your ancestor emigrated to America, it may be worth visiting *www.aisling.net/journaling/old-diaries-online.htm*. Here you will find details of the exploits of an American midwife, the poignant memories of a Virginian slave, tales of Nebraskan pioneers

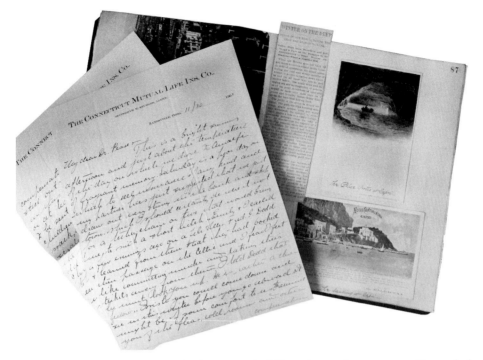

Diaries can often hold more than just handwritten entries. Tickets, photographs, newspaper cuttings and other ephemera may be pasted inside.

Examples of diary ephemera.

and the journal of a woman who spent six weeks with the Sioux Indians. Hopes, dreams, fears and excitement from the pens of ordinary men and women who have led extraordinary lives, help to give us a completely different perspective on the times when our own ancestors lived.

For those with forebears living in rural Wales in the mid-eighteenth century, some of the pages of William Bulkeley's diary are relevant and are gradually going online: visit Gathering the Jewels at *www.gtj.org.uk/en/articles/diaries-of-william-bulkeley-llanfechell-anglesey-1734-60*. Awarded a £6,500 grant, the University of Wales plans to make 1,000 handwritten pages available on the web. Bulkeley's journals consist of three volumes and cover everything from vivid accounts of farm life in Anglesey to the marriage of his daughter to a pirate.

Eyewitness accounts may take on any form, from the recollections of those aboard an 1850s whaling ship to those experiencing the effects of the Irish potato famine. Use the website *http://www.eyewitnesstohistory.com* as a basis for your own investigations.

Where documents and diaries mention specific events it is always worth trying to track down these details in local newspapers. You may be lucky and discover even more information if the incident was interesting enough to be reported.

PERFECT PENMANSHIP

Study not only the diaries and correspondence penned by your ancestor, but also the writing implement used, the quality of the paper and even their writing style, punctuation and grammar. This will not only give you clues as to the equipment they could afford, but also to their educational abilities.

Step Back in Time

The term 'pen' comes from the Latin word *penna*, meaning feather, but the origins of these writing devices date back much further. Early man chose to convey messages, make drawings and portray thoughts by using his finger as a writing device, dipped in plant juices as a primitive substitute for ink. As we developed and became civilised, more-effective tools had to be found.

Bone and bronze implements were fashioned to scratch naive images and icons onto stone, but it was the Greeks that created a writing stylus that most resembled the pen we use today. Made of metal, bone or ivory, the stylus enabled the user to make marks on hinged, wax-coated tablets that could be closed to protect the scribe's work. By 300 BC, the Chinese, as an alternative, chose to paint their messages using brushes made from rat or camel hair.

Overcoming language barriers and the opening of trade between nations required us to achieve precision and greater detail when communicating. Although the Egyptians had previously used bamboo reeds as writing tools and vessels to carry ink, it was not until after the fall of the Roman Empire that it was discovered that feather quills had greater potential. Goose feathers were most prevalent, while swan feathers, of a premium quality, were scarcer and more expensive. Crow feathers were ideal for making fine lines and doing intricate work. The hollow shaft of a feather quill acted as a reservoir to hold the ink, which flowed by capillary action to the end of the shaft, split to create a nib for writing. Popular during medieval times to write on parchment and paper to achieve a neat, controlled script, a skilled scribe could achieve numerous calligraphic effects with a well-shaped quill. But there was one drawback: each short quill would regularly need re-trimming in order to produce a sharp nib, so a constant supply of new feathers was always needed.

To overcome this problem, a tool was called for that could carry its own ink supply, was reliable and didn't require reshaping. The first steps were taken in the nineteenth century when steel nibs were produced by stamping, shaping and slitting a piece of sheet metal. These were then fitted into a holder and dipped into an inkwell to replenish the ink on the nib after every line of writing. Dickens, Austen, the Brontë sisters and their contemporaries would have all used this method to pen their novels. The holders were made from a variety of materials, including gold, silver, tortoiseshell and wood, teamed with equally elaborately decorated inkwells produced for home use, to be displayed on a desk, or as part of a travelling writing set.

Pen nibs and a pottery inkwell that would have slotted into a hole on a school desk. (Stewart Coxon)

Gradually, these advances inspired inventors to come up with a method that eliminated the constant need for dipping the nib into an inkwell.

The Fountain Pen

One of the most notable developments of late nineteenth-century writing equipment was the patenting of the reservoir fountain pen. A 'silver pen to carry ink in' was mentioned in the seventeenth century in the diaries of Samuel Pepys, but it was not until 200 years later when pens had their own reservoirs of ink that they became popular and manufacturers such as Parker, Sheaffer and Moseley brought these stylish items to the masses. They were known as 'fountain' pens in recognition of the way the ink flowed through the pen and onto the paper; a system of narrow tubes called the 'feed' carried the ink from the pen's reservoir to a gold or steel nib. Perfecting this smooth flow, without the addition of blots or irregularities, initially proved a difficult task.

By 1883 a breakthrough was made. Lewis E. Waterman, an insurance salesman, created a pen that was capable of delivering ink efficiently with his innovative 'three-channel feed' device, which allowed air to balance the pressure inside and outside the ink reservoir and stabilise the flow. The Waterman Ideal was filled using an eyedropper mechanism that sucked the ink into the pen to provide the supply. Despite leakages and teething problems with poorly fitting caps and wear to the barrel section, the pens became greatly admired by the general public.

Walter Sheaffer introduced a lever filling method where the lever fitted flush with the barrel of the pen when not in use. The Parker Pen Company patented the button-filler method as an alternative to the eyedropper system in 1913. By pressing an external button connected to the internal pressure plate, the ink sac was flattened to allow the pen to be refilled.

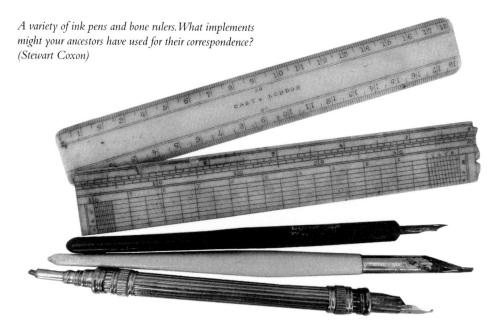

A variety of ink pens and bone rulers. What implements might your ancestors have used for their correspondence? (Stewart Coxon)

Fountain pens gradually replaced their dip-pen predecessors, allowing the user to write more quickly and with less ink spillage. The body of the pen was the perfect base for a wide variety of elaborate decoration and materials to be used. Propelling pencils also proved very popular, with their casings providing an opportunity for decoration and the option to refill them with replacement leads. (Stewart Coxon)

Top Tip If a desk drawer or box of keepsakes has presented you with a fountain pen, take the time to have a closer look at this engineering work of art. Something as simple as excessive wear to the outer barrel can tell us that this example was not only well used – probably on a daily basis in a world without computers – but also well loved.

Alongside their uses as functional objects, pens were also the perfect vehicle for decoration. Gilding, enamelling, lacquer and metal filigree work can all help to make them extremely desirable. Perhaps your discovery has prompted you to consider buying additional fountain pens. Look out for examples made before 1945 by the following manufacturers: Parker, Mabie Todd (Swan), Waterman, Montblanc, Sheaffer, Wahl Eversharp.

Condition should be your top priority:
- Avoid pens with replacement parts that have been 'made to fit'.
- Avoid damage where possible, it can be expensive to repair.
- Always buy a pen that you have seen in working order.
- Ensure that the clip on the cap is not broken.
- Check that the barrel and the cap match and whether the cap is of 'screw-on' or 'push-on' design and that it fits flush to the barrel.
- Ensure that the rubber sac or piston enables the pen to be filled with ink. If this is damaged repair can be difficult. Also check for shrinkage, distorted barrels or a generally poor working mechanism.
- Finally, examine the whole pen for cracks, discoloration and chips to the decoration.

Did You Know?

In 1980, the Writing Equipment Society was formed by a group of enthusiasts who all patronised 'His Nibs', a fascinating shop belonging to Philip Poole in Drury Lane, London. Devoting its interests to anything 'writerly' and its associated materials, the society has an international membership of over 500 followers.

Among the inkwells and seals, pen nibs and paper knives, you are guaranteed to find a like-minded member with a passion for, and considerable knowledge of, the history of these items. Members receive a journal covering the latest news, articles and advertisements as well as dates of forthcoming meetings and swap sessions. If this is an area of memorabilia that interests you, why not consider joining to find out more? Visit the website at *www.wesonline.org.uk/index.html* and take advantage of the help, guidance and links to related societies and shows.

From quill cutters to propelling pencils, along with their writing styles, the tools used by our ancestors for their correspondence can help to whittle down the time frame of those dateless examples that you may come across, possibly even helping you to match a letter with a particular individual.

Remember

These clues have literally been left in black and white. Use your imagination and logical thinking to follow them wherever they may take you.

ENCYCLOPAEDIC ALMANACS

Walk into any bookshop today and you're guaranteed to find a myriad of guides, self-help books, handbooks and manuals on just about any subject, but step back in time and the almanac was the publication you turned to, to find out important information of the day. The early Victorian era saw farming as one of the greatest employers and for those involved in this occupation, an almanac was often at hand on their bookshelves. Almanacs are published annually and contain a calendar for a given year.

Originally essential reading for farmers, almanacs listed planting dates and suggestions for the arrangements of their fields according to the calendar. They also included surprisingly accurate weather forecasts, which predicted rainfall, storms or seasonal highlights that could affect a harvest. They contained astrological information, such as the rising and setting of the sun and moon, details of forthcoming eclipses and tide tables: essential knowledge for fishermen. Like today's diary, there would be a section of 'useful information' listing the dates of important Church festivals and saints' days. The most common denominator about whatever details were included was that they dealt with the passage of time.

Roger Bacon, an English philosopher and Franciscan friar, is thought to have been the first person to use the term 'almanac' in 1267 in the context of astronomy calendars.

Almanacs in various forms have been in use for hundreds of years and were produced by numerous countries. At the height of their popularity in the seventeenth century they were second only in sales to the Bible.

British publications include:

Old Moore's Almanack Written by Francis Moore, the self-taught physician and astrologer of the court of Charles II, this astrological almanac was first published in 1697 and contained weather forecasts. Throughout the eighteenth and nineteenth centuries this pocket guide was a bestseller and is still in publication today.

Old Moore's Almanac An Irish publication in print since 1764 and originally written and produced by Theophilus Moore.

Whitaker's Almanack Published from 1868, *Whitaker's* covers a huge range of topics from peerage to politics, education to the environment. When the company headquarters were destroyed in the Blitz during the Second World War, Winston Churchill took a personal interest in ensuring that publication continued. Such was the book's popularity that in 1878, on erection of Cleopatra's Needle on the banks of London's River Thames, a time capsule was placed in the obelisk's pedestal and an almanac from that year was chosen as one of the items to be placed inside.

Wisden Cricketers' Almanack Founded in 1864 by John Wisden. During the Victorian era, the purchasing of a *Wisden Cricketers' Almanack* was essential for someone with a keen interest in the sport, educating them further on the game and allowing the owner to make their own observations. Growing from 112 pages to currently in excess of 1,500, the 75th edition produced in 1938 was marked with a change to a bright yellow cover, making it instantly recognisable in the years that followed. Previously, the covers had been buff, a lighter yellow or salmon pink. (For more information, see Chapter 15.)

Almanacs produced around a specific subject and kept by your ancestor may provide clues to hobbies, beliefs or occupations of which you had not been aware. Perhaps your ancestor chose to make a life overseas, settling in America to raise a family and work the land; if so you could seek out the American versions, which proved to be just as popular. The first official *Farmers' Almanac* was published in 1792 in New England. At this time it was common for astrologers to record their findings and sell them to interested readers, but Robert B. Thomas, editor of the publication, discovered more accurate formulas to create his recordings and weather predictions, which he presented in an entertaining and engaging manner ensuring that his almanac was an instant success.

By 1848 a new editor, John H. Jenks, had appeared on the scene and renamed the publication *The Old Farmer's Almanac*, a title that has remained to this day.

As the years passed, additional topics were covered in these much-admired pocket encyclopaedias, from changing transport methods and geographic tables to health and medical procedures such as how to let blood. Their advice and advertisements helped to spread knowledge and educate, while their illuminating passages were even read to soldiers in order to boost their morale. Whether you've inherited one of these historical gems or are interested in learning more about a particular period by purchasing your own vintage copy, then an almanac, complete with entries by the user, can give a real insight, not only into agricultural trials and tribulations but also into daily life. A census return may list the occupation of your ancestor as a 'farmer of 60 acres', but the additional information provided by an almanac about his farming methods and household accounts would be priceless.

Most useful to the family historian are the almanacs that concentrate on one particular locality, enabling us to visualise the area and the businesses established there. There were occasions when these books served a dual role as both almanac and local directory, combining the information that would often simply overlap in the individual publications. Remember to look out for almanacs that specialised in a particular subject, such as nautical and mining almanacs which are perfect for those of us with ancestors who were involved in these occupations.

What Next?

Specialised British almanacs include *The Astronomical Almanac*, published by Her Majesty's Nautical Almanac Office, which contains details of solar systems, positions of the sun and moon, times of sunrise and sunset, eclipses and astronomical reference data. The first edition of the *British Nautical Almanac and Astronomical Ephemeris*, published in 1766, contained information for the year 1767, enabling the reader to successfully calculate lunar distances in order to establish longitude at sea.

If you're not lucky enough to own a family edition, you could try to build a collection of almanacs around a specific area of interest and time frame. Only buy issues with entries that can aid your research and give a feel for a particular period. The seller should be able to enlighten you as to the general coverage of the text before you buy. If you're trying to find out more about farming life in America during the 1880s, track down examples on auction sites such as *www.ebay.co.uk* where items regularly come up for sale. Look out for those with references to the machinery used, the daily farming routines and perhaps with lists of household accounts to enable you to work out the expenses faced by someone in this occupation.

Remember

Don't be fooled into thinking that just because the entries do not apply directly to your ancestors that they are of no use to you. These forms of primary sources give a personal view of what 'real life' was like. Your mission is to expand your own family history knowledge through alternative avenues of research. An aspect covered in a diary or almanac could spur you on to find out how this particular incident, event, method or gadget had an impact on the life of your forebear.

CREATING A PRESENT OF THE PAST
FOR FUTURE GENERATIONS

The thrill of finding your forebear's hopes and fears written in their own hand cannot be beaten and the information you can glean from the pages is irreplaceable. So with that in mind, why don't you consider writing your own diary, which will be just as invaluable to your descendants and extended family in the future?

The internet and the speed of email is a tool we cannot live without but the generic, typewritten messages are often impersonal and don't really give any clues as to the personality of the writer. Yes, in the future it will be possible to print out your electronic thoughts on reams of A4 paper in times roman script but yours will look just like everybody else's. What better way to preserve your memories than to write them by hand in a diary, perhaps decorated to depict your own style, with doodles, random thoughts, additional ephemera and even the odd crossing out.

In years to come your descendants will have much more fun and excitement in discovering that perhaps you were a really artistic individual, a deep thinker, a comic or a dreamer? They will devour your handwriting for clues to your personality just as you are doing now, but with a little hindsight you can provide a greater insight into your life at the beginning of the twenty-first century.

What you include is entirely up to you, but it is worth giving it a little thought before you start. Think about the information that most excites you as a family historian. Names, dates and places are a must. Will you have a theme, perhaps recording your thoughts on various subjects close to your heart, detailing your occupation and what is involved, or a general diary on day-to-day events concerning you and your family? If you feel that you don't have the time to commit to daily jottings, compile a weekly log or sporadic journals to record holidays and travel.

Make things easier for your successors by adding details that they can follow up in years to come to find out more about you. Insert your passport number in a travel journal to enable them to research further your lifetime travels; give details of the latest gadgets of the day and most-used appliances – these could seem quaint and old-fashioned in years to come and fascinate your readers – and always include life-changing occurrences and family milestones. Brief descriptions of notable figures and historical events can provide a deeper understanding of the wider world at the time.

Remember

It may seem obvious, but always include your own name and details somewhere within the pages. It is surprising how many vintage diaries have fascinating accounts of life in another era but cannot be tied to an individual due to a lack of ownership information, resulting in a family's stories being lost to them forever.

TWO

TRAVEL AND TRANSPORT

*I never travel without my diary. One should always have
something sensational to read on the train.*

Oscar Wilde

This chapter follows on from the previous theme of diaries in general to concentrate on the specialist area of travel diaries, journals and related memorabilia.

We can often be mistaken in thinking that it was only in the latter part of the twentieth century that we started travelling the globe in earnest. Yes, there are many occasions when our ancestors were born, married and buried in the same village and never strayed far outside it, but there are thousands of other instances when the lure of adventure saw them journey far and wide.

Travel was not solely for the rich – although the ways in which they made their journeys often differed considerably – and many poorer families ended up far from their original birthplace. The search for a better life, the promise of escaping the conditions they had found themselves in and the motivation to find better housing and jobs to support their families were just some of the contributing factors. This could involve moving within the British Isles, such as during the Industrial Revolution when people moved from the country to the flourishing towns and cities for employment, but could also include movement further afield when the living conditions in these areas prompted them to seek new opportunities overseas. Before planes, trains and automobiles, the ship was the only option for those who wished to venture further from our shores. To understand this migration and the physical reminders these trips may have produced we must travel back through the decades to find out more.

Step Back in Time

In 1788, the British First Fleet of penal transportation ships arrived in Australia to establish a penal colony at Sydney Cove. This fledgling settlement was named the Colony of New South Wales. At the time, the country had an Aboriginal population of approximately 400,000 people, but between 1788 and 1840, 80,000 convicts from Britain and its colonies 'invaded' when they were deported to Australia for punishment. There soon became the need for free settlers to fill the jobs that were created, but attracting newcomers was difficult due to the travel costs, which were much higher than those involved in migrating to America. Some people used their own resources while others needed assistance from the limited schemes that were in place. Initially, land prices were kept high in order to use the money to subsidise the travelling expenses of potential settlers.

The following decade saw a reversal of events when a flood of Europeans disembarked in Australia hoping to seek their fortune. In 1851 gold had been discovered just outside Bathurst and the Gold Rush began in earnest as people fought to stake their claim. Over the next ten years, 600,000 immigrants arrived, many settling in this 'new' continent for good, raising families and increasing the population.

Another million people arrived in the country between 1860 and 1900, by which time assistance schemes and immigration policies were helping to control and maintain the levels of newcomers.

IN NEED OF ASSISTANCE?

For voluntary settlers there were two ways in which they could travel, either as assisted passengers, who had all or part of their passage paid for them, or as unassisted passengers, who funded their own trip.

Assisted passengers

During the nineteenth century, there were a variety of reasons why people wished to emigrate. Besides the obvious lure of the Gold Rush, many wanted to escape the poverty, unemployment and hardships that their lives involved in Britain. For the Irish, the potato famine had left families decimated and the possibility of a new start was all the more appealing, whereas other emigrants hoped to escape the fear of persecution brought on by their nationalities and find a place to settle.

Those wishing to emigrate to the southern hemisphere also faced the prospect of not earning wages for the length of the journey and the period of settlement once they reached their destination. This category usually included farm labourers and domestic servants. British governments were eager to populate their overseas colonies and provided grants or tempted others to move by offering farmland in the 'new world' at a cheap rate. One such scheme took place in New Zealand when the Canterbury Association was formed to establish an Anglican colony in the country and resulted in a dozen immigrant ships leaving Britain for the new settlement in the 1850s.

Liverpool was one of the locations from which many travellers departed; it was already well established as a port due to its transatlantic links and trade in cotton and timber. Most passengers would spend a short period in the city before their ship was due to sail, often staying in one of a host of boarding houses that benefited from this passing trade.

Before the 1860s, sailing ships would leave the dockside on a journey that would last anything between three and four months. Once on board, the poorest passengers

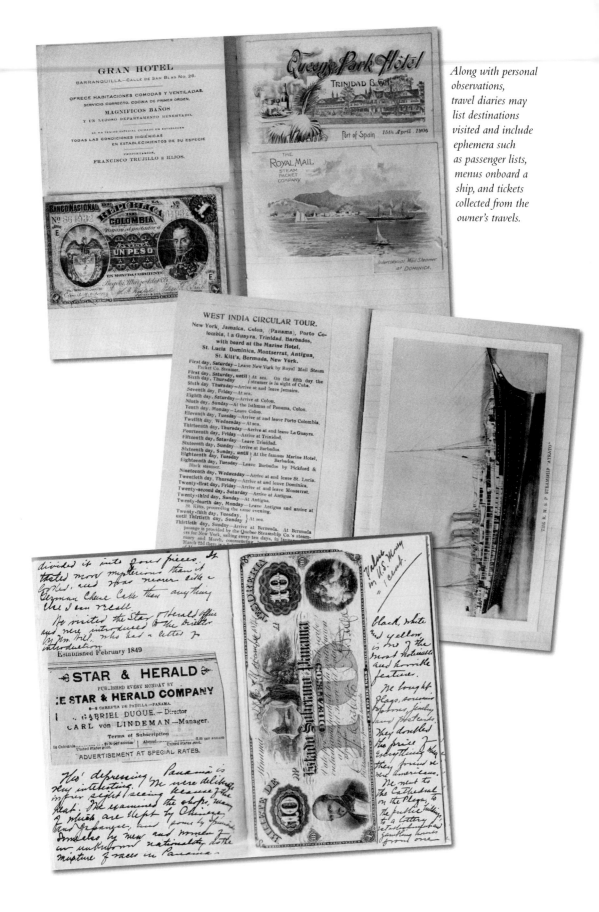

GRAN HOTEL

BARRANQUILLA.—CALLE DE SAN BLAS No. 26.

OFRECE HABITACIONES COMODAS Y VENTILADAS.

SERVICIO CORRECTO. COCINA DE PRIMER ORGEN.

MAGNIFICOS BAÑOS

Y UN LUJOSO DEPARTAMENTO RESERVADO.

SE HA TENIDO ESPECIAL CUIDADO EN ESTABLECER

TODAS LAS CONDICIONES HIGIENICAS

EN ESTABLECIMIENTOS DE SU ESPECIE

PROPIETARIOS,

FRANCISCO TRUJILLO E HIJOS.

Queen's Park Hotel
TRINIDAD B.W.I.

Port of Spain   15th April 1906

THE
ROYAL MAIL
STEAM
PACKET
COMPANY

Intercolonial Mail Steamer at DOMINICA.

Along with personal observations, travel diaries may list destinations visited and include ephemera such as passenger lists, menus onboard a ship, and tickets collected from the owner's travels.

WEST INDIA CIRCULAR TOUR.

New York, Jamaica, Colon, (Panama), Porto Colombia, La Guayra, Trinidad, Barbados, with board at the Marine Hotel, St. Lucia Dominica, Montserrat, Antigua, St. Kitt's, Bermuda, New York.

First day, Saturday—Leave New York by Royal Mail Steam Packet Co. Steamer.

First day, Saturday, until } At sea. On the fifth day the
Sixth day, Thursday } steamer is in sight of Cuba.

Sixth day, Thursday—Arrive at and leave Jamaica.

Seventh day, Friday—At sea.

Eighth day, Saturday—Arrive at Colon.

Ninth day, Sunday—At the Isthmus of Panama, Colon.

Tenth day, Monday—Leave Colon.

Eleventh day, Tuesday—Arrive at and leave Porto Colombia.

Twelfth day, Wednesday—At sea.

Thirteenth day, Thursday—Arrive at and leave La Guayra.

Fourteenth day, Friday—Arrive at Trinidad.

Fifteenth day, Saturday—Leave Trinidad.

Sixteenth day, Sunday—Arrive at Barbados.

Sixteenth day, Sunday, until } At the famous Marine Hotel,
Eighteenth day, Tuesday } Barbados.

Eighteenth day, Tuesday—Leave Barbados by Pickford & Black steamer.

Nineteenth day, Wednesday—Arrive at and leave St. Lucia.

Twentieth day, Thursday—Arrive at and leave Dominica.

Twenty-first day, Friday—Arrive at and leave Mousserat.

Twenty-second day, Saturday—Arrive at Antigua.

Twenty-third day, Sunday—At Antigua.

Twenty-fourth day, Monday—Leave Antigua and arrive at St. Kitts, proceeding the same evening.

Twenty-fifth day, Tuesday, } At sea.
until Thirtieth day, Sunday }

Thirtieth day, Sunday—Arrive at Bermuda. At Bermuda passage is provided by the Quebec Steamship Co.'s steamers for New York, sailing every ten days, in January and March, commencing March 22d then in ...

Established February 1849

STAR & HERALD

PUBLISHED EVERY MONDAY BY

THE STAR & HERALD COMPANY

8 CARRERA DE PADILLA—PANAMA.

GABRIEL DUQUE.—Director

CARL von LINDEMAN—Manager.

Terms of Subscription

In Colombia ... $ 6.00 per annum   Abroad .... $ 8.00 per annum
United States gold.   United States gold.

ADVERTISEMENT AT SPECIAL RATES.

divided it into four pieces. It tasted more mysterious than it looked, and was nearer like a German Cheese Cake than anything else I can recall.

We visited the Star & Herald office and were introduced to the director by Mr. Hill, who had a letter of introduction.

Tho' depressing, Panama is very interesting. We were delighted in our sight seeing because of the heat. We examined the shops, many of which are kept by Chinese and Japanese, and some by French. Some also by men and women of unknown nationality. So the mixture of races in Panama.

Value in U.S. Money "1 Cent."

Black, white and yellow, is one of the most noticeable and horrible features. We bought flags, souvenir spoons, jewelry and postcards. They doubled the price of everything when they found we were Americans. We went to the Cathedral on the Plaza, to the public building to a lottery establishment — gambling hones from one...

would be allotted the cheapest accommodation, in steerage class. This took the form of a crowded dormitory with bunks stacked around the outside and a central area of tables in the middle. The damp and claustrophobic conditions meant that they spent a great deal of their time huddled on deck, no matter what the weather conditions; they faced a combination of stormy seas and sweltering heat, with very little shelter from either.

Lack of ventilation and sanitary conditions meant disease was rife. Cases of typhoid and cholera spread through these areas and although the infected decks were confined in an effort to control the outbreaks, many passengers died without ever reaching the 'promised land'.

Conditions gradually began to improve after the introduction of the Passenger Act in 1855, which required minimum standards for ventilation, sanitation, the amount of space allotted and food rations provided. Steam ships, which reduced the length and cost of the journey, started to replace sailing ships and the companies began to offer a complete travel package to their customers, which included decent accommodation before sailing and better facilities onboard, although it wasn't until the 1900s that steerage was replaced with third-class cabins.

Free passages were sometimes granted for those who were particularly required in the country and could not pay their own fare, such as married couples without children or female domestic servants. Stipulations were such that applicants had to pay one pound for each adult and intend to reside permanently in the colony.

A naturalised settler or citizen born in the colony could apply for a 'passage warrant' for a friend or relative in Britain to join them. Once presented with the warrant, the government could then arrange the emigration procedure: this was known as a Remittance or Nominated Passage. A similar process was arranged if an employer wanted a particular employee from Europe. The employer would pay the government a percentage of the fare and the government would engage the labour on his behalf. Once the employee arrived they would be classed as an indentured immigrant and would be 'legally' bound to work for the employer for a set period of time.

What Next?

If you know that one of your ancestors emigrated to Australia during the mid to late Victorian era then why not try to find out more? Collect together any information, documents, letters and ephemera and try to establish a time frame and location, working backwards from your known and confirmed facts. Research sea voyages and transportation at this time to understand the conditions they would have faced during the trip and also when they arrived. Try to establish from living relatives what factors prompted them to leave for a life overseas. This decision could well have been paramount in establishing the direction your family tree took in subsequent generations.

By typing 'assisted immigrants' in the top toolbar at *www.records.nsw.gov.au* you will be directed to numerous pages giving details of how to search for assisted passengers. Dates of embarkation, ports of arrival and names of the vessels are listed on these indexes and there is also information concerning how to access the records, as well as details on how to employ a researcher to help.

TRAVELLING UNDER YOUR OWN STEAM

Unassisted passengers

Towards the end of the nineteenth century, London was also a popular departure point for larger vessels on these long-distance journeys. Barques, clipper ships and steamers all populated the waters.

Tilbury Docks opened in 1886 with luxury accommodation situated nearby in the Tilbury Hotel where wealthy passengers could while away the time before they travelled. Although a distinctive design, many disliked the way the building stood out. Writer Joseph Conrad described it as, 'a shapeless and desolate red edifice' and condemned its 'monstrous ugliness'. Could your ancestor have stayed in this or a similar hotel before their journey? Did they keep any leaflets or paper ephemera as a memento of their time there?

Once onboard, standards were high. Even in 1853, there are reports of numerous stewards to attend to the passengers in first class, and comfortable accommodation, recreational and dining facilities. For those a little less wealthy, messmen were elected to receive the provisions for the week from the purser, and these were then given out to the passengers in the second and lower classes. These intermediate passengers also had to provide their own utensils, dishes and tins to hold their supplies. A daily allocation of 3 pints of fresh water was given to each adult with a further 3 pints given to the cook to make each passenger's soups, stews or hot drinks. Salt and molasses were used as preservatives and featured regularly in the menu as 'salt beef' or 'porridge with molasses'. Oatcakes and bread were handed out throughout the week but also rationed. Set mealtimes were strictly adhered to and each 'mess' ate at separate times to ensure that passengers received their fair share of rations from their messman.

Two small (or one large) items of luggage was allowed onboard per passenger. One was placed in the hold until they arrived at their destination, while the other was used to store their belongings throughout the journey. Certain days were set aside for washing clothes, which were then hung from the rigging to dry.

A bell was struck at 10 p.m. to signal lights-out and from that time onwards, passengers were not allowed to make any noise so that they did not disturb those in bed. Anyone not wishing to go to sleep at this time had to remain on deck. From 6 a.m., the doctor would carry out his rounds to ensure that all passengers had risen, especially in hot weather.

Old currency may indicate countries visited by our forebears. Do your research to establish when the particular design of banknote was in circulation to help work out when it may have been collected.

Time inevitably improved conditions and procedures, but compared to their assisted counterparts, wealthy unassisted passengers were in a league of their own. Those with means often chose to travel for their health, to visit relatives already settled in the New World or to pursue employment opportunities. Their accommodation varied, with some passengers even able to choose their cabins before departure.

What Next?

Even if your own forebears have not left diaries detailing their trips, there are hundreds of others who did. Auction houses, dealers specialising in paper memorabilia and websites like *www.ebay.co.uk* regularly sell these exceptional finds, which are unique and can often be quite affordable. Their content can help you understand life aboard ship, the conditions endured and the sights and experiences that would have been new and novel to them at the time. Shipping companies may be mentioned, which could give you a direct link to the same type of vessel on which your ancestor travelled, while a general feel for a different era can be gleaned from these first-hand accounts.

CASE STUDY I

THE GOLDEN AGE OF SAIL

Messrs Devitt and Moore were owners of just one of the shipping owners operating its vessels on the route from Britain to Australia and New Zealand from 1863 and were rated highly as some of the pioneers in the passenger trade of South Australia.

One noteworthy ship was the SS *Rodney*. Built in 1874, this full-rigged clipper was constructed from iron and fitted out for the comfort of its passengers.

A personal diary that survived from one unassisted passenger from 1891 gives us a glimpse into how easy it was to travel if you had the money available and how you can use the information contained within a personal journal for new and exciting lines of enquiry.

Monday 11 May 1891

Having decided to travel to Australia in a sailing ship I journeyed to the East India Docks on Wednesday the 6th May 1891 and inspected the full rigged Clipper Packet Ship 'Rodney'. 3000 ton burthen and classed 100 A1 at Lloyds belonging to Messers Devitt and Moore of London. Several berths were disengaged and the steward showed me over the vessel.

I made up my mind that I would not travel by her unless I had a good cabin to myself for a single fare (£52.10.0) and after some trouble at the office of the Agents (Messers Green and Co), I succeeded in securing a cabin (No 3) on the port side measuring 9ft 7in by 8ft 2 in.

Just from the details in these two simple paragraphs, further background research tells us that the ship was able to accommodate sixty people in two-berth first-class cabins up to 10ft square. These compartments were equipped with fitted lavatory basins and chests of drawers, regarded as extreme luxuries for the day. Communal bathrooms were also available on board with the added selling point of both hot and cold water, itself a novelty as previously only cold water had been available in the washing facilities.

An 80ft-long saloon provided a place to socialise and relax and a sanctuary where women could read or sew, sheltered from the weather outside. In most ships of this type, the saloon was well lit and decorated to a high standard, often with images of the destinations where the vessels were bound. A piano was accessible to provide entertainment and the furniture could be pushed back to allow room for dancing. Stained glass, carved woodwork and plush upholstery would have been the norm, and would have been expected by her paying passengers.

For the men, a smoker's room was located near the companionway where they could smoke (without upsetting the females who found it distasteful) and discuss events of the day: a male domain providing escape from the confines of the ship.

Take these nuggets of information to the next level by using your research skills to look at documentary resources such as newspapers. Here, an account of the vessel when new was found in an Australian newspaper from 1874 describing what could be expected on board:

> The worry and bother of attending to the fitting up, as well as the extra expenditure of time and money, are now avoided, and with very little need for previous provision of preparation, the intending voyager can step on board ship and find his cabin carpeted and fitted up with almost all the accessories and appointments of a bedroom in a hotel.

It even mentions the added amenities of 'good-sized looking-glasses and handy little racks for water bottles, tumblers, combs and brushes'.

As well as the berths for first-class travellers there was also the area between decks for second-class and steerage passengers, which was well ventilated and provided adequate standards for those with a little less money to spend. The galley of the *Rodney* was able to feed 500 people when necessary and as such she was considered one of the most elegant and amenable vessels of her day, not to mention one of the fastest.

Letters from captains of ships during the 1840s, 50s and 60s help us to understand what life was like onboard during this period and the types of cargo carried. Remember that not all correspondence has to belong to your ancestors for you to gain an insight into what their life in similar circumstances would have been like.

By comparing other regulations and requirements of the period it becomes apparent that speed was of the essence at this time and shipping companies fought to provide a quick, trouble-free and efficient service to encourage both repeat and potential customers. Sailing in both the same period and along the same route as the *Cutty Sark*, the *Rodney* had some stiff competition. She made her best passage to Sydney in 1887 in sixty-eight days, and from Sydney to London in seventy-seven days in 1890 – just pipped to the post by the *Cutty Sark,* which had arrived four days previously.

From entries in this diary and others from a similar period it is evident that at the mercy of weather and sea conditions, these voyages relied on the skills of the captain and crew, but the passengers' lives were often in the hands of the gods. Tugs and pilot boats would help guide the clipper ships in and out of the docks, creating a great spectacle for the passengers on deck who would sometimes place bets on which hour the pilot master would come aboard to take over, or at what precise time they would dock: a little light entertainment after a hazardous voyage.

Consider

From the memorabilia you have found, ask yourself the following questions before you embark on your quest to build up an intriguing collection that showcases your ancestor's travels.

* Try to clarify with background research the era in which your ancestor was travelling and the purpose: was it a business trip, holiday or emigration?
* Are there specific items that could bring their adventures to life, such as a picture of the vessel, advertising memorabilia and documentation of the voyage, commemorative wares from a particular shipping line which feature its insignia, period photographs of the locations visited en route?

Perhaps you've inherited a tattered newspaper clipping with the name of your forebear mentioned in an article about a ship's arrival in port. It is interesting to note that until 1854, many unassisted passengers who travelled by steerage class were not listed separately in any passenger lists. Newspapers of the day often reported the arrival of ships, and passenger details can sometimes be found in them. Contact the State Library of New South Wales, *www.sl.nsw.gov.au*, to see if copies for the year you require still exist and follow the 'About the Collections' link to the newspaper section.

Even a simple entry mentioning a particular shipping company can provide clues as to the reasons for travel. Regular immigrant ship companies operating from Liverpool included Shaw, Savill and Albion, which ran cargo and passenger services to New Zealand from 1882 and purchased surplus White Star Line steamer ships to use on this route from 1883. You can research the ships of the White Star Line and Shaw, Savill and Albion Line at *www.theshipslist.com/ships/lines/shaw.html*. Harland and Wolff's archives can be located at *www.proni.gov.uk* (the Public Record Office of Northern Ireland); type Harland and Wolff into the search engine to bring up their holdings. Previously, the Black Ball Line of Liverpool had dominated the Australian passage with its fleet of packet ships set up by James Baines and Co. in 1852. Carrying emigrants and cargo during the Gold Rush era, its first vessel, *Marco Polo*, set the record for the quickest round trip, giving the company a reputation for fast passages. The eagerness with which people wanted to reach the gold fields not only encouraged the building of faster ships but also led to an improvement in the state of the accommodation and provisions onboard. Visit *www.liverpoolmuseums.org.uk/maritime/archive* to research the Liverpool-based transatlantic liners or the Liverpool Record Office at *www.liverpool.gov.uk/archives* for other shipping companies.

Once you have discovered the vessel on which your ancestor sailed, you will be able to establish the shipping company and research any additional information that survives at the Maritime or National Archives. See Case Study 2 for a more in-depth look at travel aboard Royal Mail Steam Packet ships.

Unfortunately, it was sometimes the case that not all passengers survived the voyage. Although the vessels would have had a doctor on board, illness and disease could often be a problem and the lack of medical supplies could result in the death of a passenger no matter how luxurious the accommodation. In this instance there was no option but for the captain to record the event with the aid of witnesses so that he could report the event once the ship had docked. Due to the length of the voyage, the person who had passed away would be buried at sea after a short committal service on deck. These were sad occasions and did nothing to boost the morale of the other passengers and crew on board who had often become a small community in the time they were at sea. These unfortunate events were often documented in the journals of those onboard, many of whom had never witnessed this type of burial before.

Have you inherited an old suitcase, once used on your ancestor's travels but now perhaps a repository for your family ephemera? (Stewart Coxon)

What Next?

To begin tracing British passengers who have died at sea, start at The National Archives website, *www.nationalarchives.gov.uk*, and follow the links under the heading 'Births, Marriages and Deaths'. *Findmypast.co.uk* also has a searchable online database of deaths at sea between 1854 and 1890. You may discover family letters describing the birth or marriage of an ancestor during the voyage. At *www.findmypast.co.uk* you can search for births at sea between 1854 and 1887, and marriages between 1854 and 1908.

CASE STUDY 2

STEAMING AHEAD

Not all of us are fortunate enough to inherit a travel item that relates directly to our ancestors, but you can glean a huge amount from similar ephemera and documents of the period. When I was trying to find out more about the Royal Mail Steam Packet ships and their voyages at the beginning of the 1900s, I bought a travel journal written by a young female traveller that enabled me to fill in a back story of those who had taken similar trips at this time. To establish to whom the journal belonged, a little detective work was needed after I discovered that the owner had conveniently drawn a dining-room seating plan on one of the pages. With the help of the passenger list, I managed to match the initials to the names of those onboard. Use similar techniques and lateral thinking to sort out any identity problems you may come across with your own examples: the smallest clues within the text or an image could help you establish names, dates and facts as well as possibly attributing the piece to its owner.

Today, Cunard, P&O Cruises and Royal Caribbean are just some of the operators that take us to far-flung destinations, but during the late nineteenth and early twentieth century, Royal Mail Steam Packets were the vessels of choice. Carry out a little background research and your understanding will grow.

On 26 September 1839 a Royal Charter was granted by Queen Victoria that allowed mail to be conveyed by the newly formed Royal Mail Steam Packet Company (RMSP) between Great Britain, the West Indies, North America, South America and other foreign ports. The operation was more costly than anyone had anticipated, so to increase profits mail liners were introduced, carrying refrigerated cargoes and passengers in first-class accommodation, to various ports along their routes.

My journal takes up the story from the viewpoint of a Miss M.E. Haines, aboard the RMSP ship *Atrato*, departing from New York on Sunday 1 April 1906.

Miss Haines was travelling alone, intending to improve her health before reaching Bermuda where she was to be married. This voyage was known as the West Indian

Circular Tour and included stops at Jamaica, Colón (Panama), Puerto Colombia, La Guaira, Trinidad, Barbados, St Lucia, Dominica, Montserrat, Antigua, St Kitts and Bermuda before returning to New York. The route had first extended to Colón in 1868 and it was now a regular destination on this trip.

The diary includes the RMSP Company's original itinerary, featuring the sales pitch: 'New York round to New York, including meals and berth and first class passage, and board at the Marine Hotel for a period of not more than three days while awaiting the connecting steamer to Barbados'. This trip was expected to take thirty days, all for the very reasonable fare of $172.00.

Furnishings on the ships were often described as luxurious in the promotional literature of the time, with electric fans installed to keep the passengers cool in the tropical heat. Exquisite decoration, attention to detail and spacious staterooms ensured that the leisurely trips between the Caribbean islands were enjoyed by those onboard. During the day, shore and launch excursions allowed time in each port and in the evenings, dinner and entertainment would take place, which included dancing on deck or music in the salon.

Miss Haines vividly describes the other passengers, giving a feel for the class of people who were able to afford these cruises and the atmosphere onboard during that period.

At Kingston we added to our list – General Caulfield and Colonel Mills of the English Army, who are on a tour of inspection of colonial forces and will be with us for a few days… Mr West – is a moving picture man who is intending to give lectures in England and another man in the same business – Mr E.T. Hutchens of Philadelphia – is going into the interior of South America for films… Mr Wilson is a mining engineer and the Duggan's are charming people – he is not practising medicine now but travelling for his health.

Her entries provide evocative images of early twentieth-century travel and the backgrounds of fellow passengers. Although diary descriptions are purely personal, they do give first-hand accounts of what destinations were like at the time. For our ancestors, it could seem as though they had stepped into a different world and their vivid explanations can be testimony to that. For example, today the Panama Canal is considered a fantastic feat of engineering, but sadly, Miss Haines was not too impressed with the area in 1906:

Colon is the Atlantic seaport of the new republic of Panama. This is an awful place! Amongst the interesting glimpses we caught were little boys skipping around in nature's own garb … most of the buildings are very attractive built on stilts so water cannot collect underneath and breed mosquitoes. Tho' depressing, Panama is very interesting. We examined the shops, many of which are kept by Chinese and Japanese and bought flags and souvenirs, spoons, jewellery and postcards.

Just part of a unique insight into the thoughts of a lone woman traveller in the early 1900s.

BUILDING A BIGGER PICTURE

So just where do you start when trying to create a collection to best demonstrate the Royal Mail Steam Packet lines? A wealth of memorabilia is available for this company, including postcards and images of the vessels. A search of the auction website *www.ebay.co.uk* lists a wide selection featuring numerous views of the ships from the *Aragon* to the *Andes*. A nearly complete list of the ships and various routes travelled can be found at *www.theshipslist.com/ships/lines/royalmail.html*.

In the early 1900s, Raphael Tuck produced different series of artist-signed postcards for the RMSP Company, enabling passengers to write home on stationery illustrated with the places where they had docked. These are extremely sought after and carry the company logo on the back of each card.

Look out for other postal items that have been posted direct from the ship – with the oval stamp stating 'Posted from the High Seas' – or en route with stamps from the countries visited during the voyage.

I came across a plan of the RMSP *Atlantis* that gave details of a cruise taken from Southampton in February 1932, stating the price of cabins in guineas and the layout onboard ship. Details of the deck plans are surrounded with photographic images of the facilities available and the ship at anchor in one of the many ports.

Examples of advertising can make your collection come alive, ranging from black and white images with detailed text to bright and colourful illustrations tempting travellers to visit exotic shores. Full-page spreads in *Punch*, the *London Charivari*, *The Illustrated London News* and other publications of the day provide clues to which ships were sailing during a particular period and the routes they were taking.

For those interested in numismatics, why not track down currency from the period like the foresighted Miss Haines, who collected the local currency and pasted examples in her diary. The banknotes from the early twentieth century from Colombia, Venezuela and the West Indies form an intriguing collection on their own, with their intricate etching and unusual imagery. They can create a bigger picture of the countries visited during each cruise and may even lead to a sideline amassing the stamps and related postal items of specific destinations.

Today, we love taking mementoes home from our trips and this is an area that should not be overlooked in your own collection. A brief search of internet items for sale shows original brass buttons with the RMSP logo embossed on them and even cutlery embellished with the company mark.

The world's postal system is a fascinating and diverse subject and it only needs a little thought to discover an area of it that could make an unusual and affordable collection that will be of interest for generations to come. Use the above techniques to compile items related to the vessels sailed and countries visited by those in your family tree.

BRITISH HOLIDAYING HERITAGE

Perhaps your ancestors weren't interested in emigrating but simply wanted a break from the rigours of working life? Numerous hot spots around our coastline became the places to see and be seen as people enjoyed the sea air and even took the waters for their health. Long before short-haul flights abroad, we Brits liked to roll up our sleeves, turn up our trousers legs and even don our bathing suits when we holidayed at home.

Before the nineteenth century, taking a holiday was a pastime favoured only by the wealthy upper classes. It was fashionable for young men, and young women accompanied by a guardian or chaperone, to take off on what was known as the Grand Tour. Visiting European cities, they would take in all the famous sights in order to expand their knowledge of art, culture, traditions and customs, returning to the UK refreshed, with new ideas and in some cases, even a spouse.

For those who preferred a change of scene on British soil, spa towns such as Bath, Tunbridge Wells, Royal Leamington and Harrogate all provided the perfect retreat for anyone who needed to rest and recuperate from a particular ailment or simply to socialise with others from a similar background. Spa towns offered hydrotherapy, which involved bathing and drinking waters from a natural spring as well as having cold water or mineral treatments and thermal baths that were believed to restore health after illness. This practice coined the phrase 'taking the waters' and evolved from the early religious pilgrimages to the sites of holy waters and the later recommendations of doctors who preached the medicinal benefits of drinking sea water.

The working classes were not so fortunate and usually only had one day off a week, which was intended for church-going and time with the family. The development of the railways in the early 1830s saw the working classes gradually begin to use Wake's Week as an opportunity to travel affordably around Britain to seaside resorts to enjoy a *proper* holiday. Wake's Week was a former religious festival, adapted in the industrial era to create a regular summer break when the cotton mills would close to give their workers time off.

In the summer of 1841, former Baptist preacher Thomas Cook hit upon the idea of improving the dreary lives of the working classes by guiding them away from alcohol through education. Cook organised a special train to take a group of Leicester temperance supporters to a meeting in Loughborough and was thrilled with the success of what became a great social event and day out.

Over the next three years he arranged numerous other trips and by 1845 felt confident enough to organise an outing to Liverpool that included low-cost rail tickets and a handbook detailing the journey, which became the forerunner of today's holiday brochure. He went on to use the Great Exhibition of 1851 as a showcase for his tours, initially bringing people down to Crystal Palace and then encouraging them to take other tours in Scotland, Ireland and Wales before branching out further afield to locations in Europe and beyond.

What Next?

If your ancestor travelled on a Thomas Cook tour find out more about the history of this institution, key dates and links to its archives at *www.thomascook.com/about-us/thomas-cook-history*. Add to your memorabilia with related Thomas Cook items by searching auction sites such as *www.ebay.co.uk*, seeking out paper ephemera at antiques and book fairs, or tracking down original newspaper advertisements in old publications such as *The Graphic*, *The Sphere* or *The Illustrated London News*.

Did You Know?

The Temperance Movement

Popular in Britain in the nineteenth century, the temperance movement was introduced to advocate the moderation or abstention of alcohol. One of the movement's founding fathers was Joseph William Livesey (1794–1884) from Preston who, along with seven other working men, signed a pledge of total abstinence. From humble beginnings the organisation quickly gathered momentum and within a year, the first temperance hotel was opened in 1833 followed by the successful *Preston Temperance Advocate* magazine, which ran from 1834–7.

Livesey was a dedicated social reformer, politician and campaigner who fought hard for the British Association for the Promotion of Temperance to be introduced in 1835. With the help of supporters such as John Turner, the phrase 'teetotal' was coined requiring the promise not to drink any form of alcohol, including spirits, wine and beer, or to provide it to others. Rousing speeches engaged the working classes into considering that abstinence would give them an air of respectability as they fought for the right to vote.

It wasn't only men who were encouraged to join. In 1847, an organisation called the Band of Hope was set up in Leeds to teach working-class children the 'evils of drink' and enrolling youngsters from the age of 6 to listen to weekly lectures and participate in activities that would steer them away from the temptation of alcohol. In 1876, the British Women's Temperance Association was formed in an attempt to stop their menfolk drinking.

Although the movement attempted to pressurise the government into implementing anti-alcohol legislation, it was never put into operation like America's prohibition laws. Politicians were lobbied to reduce the Sunday opening hours of public houses. The Salvation Army, Quakers and some Catholic organisations tried to persuade them to ban or restrict alcohol sales, but no large-scale plan was ever adopted in Britain despite the National Temperance Federation being set up in association with the Liberal Party in 1884.

*Temperance memorabilia: a certificate of merit awarded by
the Liverpool Church of England Temperance Society.
The 'Junior Division' indicates that practices
were taught from a young age.*

Nonconformists tended to be active in the temperance movement, with about one-tenth of the adult population believed to be abstainers from alcohol by 1900.

By the First World War restrictions were introduced as a direct result of the conflict and the new Defence of the Realm Act in 1914. Some breweries were nationalised or transformed into munitions factories, reducing the alcohol supply available, and taxes were raised by an extra penny a pint, alcohol content moderated and pub hours subjected to license.

Areas, street names and buildings can all hold a key to Britain's temperance past. Dog Kennel Lane, site of the former Manchester F.C. football stadium, was renamed Maine Road by members of the temperance movement in recognition of the Maine Law passed in the US in 1851 that stated that alcohol should be prohibited except for 'medicinal, mechanical or manufacturing purposes'. By 1855, this law had spread to twelve states and brought about the term 'dry' state; those without prohibition laws were known as 'wet' states.

Was your ancestor involved in the temperance movement? Physical clues to look out for are propaganda leaflets and literature detailing the cause, certificates confirming entry into the movement and ceramics decorated with uplifting messages such as 'Temperance is the parent of sobriety, happiness, health etc.'. Smaller items like Band of

Hope badges, medals and fobs may have found their way into old jewellery boxes and postcards of temperance hotels could point to establishments that your ancestor may have visited.

MEMENTOES AND MEMORIES

During the 1800s, it became a tradition to take home a souvenir of your trip. The Victorians were known for being hoarders and it was fashionable for their homes to be filled with trinkets and ornaments, clustered together on shelves and tables to decorate their rooms. There was often no format to their tastes; most just collected the pieces they liked or that were memorable to a person, occasion or trip they had taken.

The word 'souvenir' comes from the French word for 'remember' and although the late Victorians enjoyed the tradition of bringing a memento home from their British seaside holidays, the practice continued well into the 1900s, reaching its peak in the 1950s when specific items, often cheap and cheerful in appearance, were produced for the tourist market.

Despite this, the custom was not invented by the Victorians and instead had been around for many centuries. Early Christian pilgrims returning from the Holy Land would buy trinkets from the merchants who plied their trade around the holy sites, in the belief that they would protect them on their dangerous journey home. Just like today, these merchants had a sales pitch selling pieces of animal bone as remnants of a saint's finger or toe, or small segments of wood said to be splinters from the original cross on which Christ was crucified. These were then brought back, shown to others and proudly displayed in the pilgrim's local church or place of worship.

From the sixteenth century onwards, Brits with a large disposable income enjoyed the adventure of what was to become known as the Grand Tour, where they would leave our shores, often for many months, in search of adventure and culture in Europe. As they travelled from city to city they would clock up an itinerary of places such as Rome, Paris, Florence and Venice, then some would venture further afield to Egypt and the treasures of the Nile. Soaking up the atmosphere, they would purchase arte-facts from excavation sites, with many of these precious goods leaving their point of origin to eventually find new homes in cabinets and display cases back in Britain. There were no restrictions on removal as there are today and even if these excavated items were not blatantly sold, many still managed to find their way into the luggage of the travellers along with marble-inlaid tables, paintings, glass and bronze statues, bringing a little bit of European style back to Britain. Visit any stately home to see the wealth of items that were collected along the way.

But you don't have to have the luxury of a stately pile to your name to have inher-ited or come across unusual examples of tourist trade mementoes.

Closer to home you may have had an ancestor who attended the Great Exhibition held at the Crystal Palace, London, in May 1851. As an organiser, exhibitor or visitor it was realised that everyone would enjoy taking home a souvenir of their trip and a variety of items were produced with this in mind. The exhibition was staged at the end of the Industrial Revolution and was an opportunity for inventors and manufacturers to show just what Britain was capable of producing. Techniques that had been mastered at that time, such as transfer printing on pottery and porcelain, the lithographic printing of images and various mechanical innovations found their way into the souvenir market.

It was possible to purchase lithographic prints of the Great Exhibition hall, transfer-printed commemorative ceramics and other exhibition souvenirs. Tucked away in your ancestor's possessions you may have discovered a small card that unfolded to show a 3D view of the exhibition halls – this was known as a Panorama. Don't fall into the trap of dismissing items such as these as pretty little novelties.

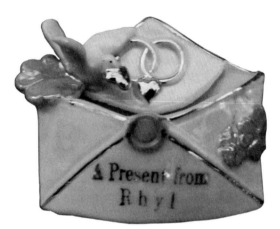

Small ceramic souvenirs were popular purchases with late Victorian and early Edwardian holidaymakers and were a lasting reminder of the destinations they had visited. Does your family memorabilia give clues to your ancestor's favourite holiday hotspot? (Stewart Coxon)

Ask yourself:

* How are these pieces connected to your past and how did they come into your ancestor's possession?
* If the piece commemorates an event or occasion, could your ancestor have attended? Look for more clues and ask probing questions of your family members to try and find out more. A chance remark or memory could hold the key.
* Research the event further, confirm the dates on which it took place and try to create a simple timeline so that you can pinpoint which ancestors were around at that time and available to attend. The Festival of Britain in 1951, royal visits to local towns, the launching of a new ship, the journey of a new train, or the inauguration of a prime minister or monarch may all have prompted your ancestors to plan a trip around these momentous occasions, resulting in them collecting memorabilia and souvenirs along the way.

Of course, your ancestors are also just as likely to have taken a trip for no other reason than pleasure and a well-earned break from work. The introduction of the railways enabled people to journey to the coast with their family to enjoy a few days in the bracing air of the British seaside. A wide range of souvenirs, affordable to the workin man or woman's pocket, were produced and were often ceramic based such as mugs, dishes, vases and small plates. Knick-knacks, shell-ware and small ornaments were highly collectable without breaking the bank and provided a lasting reminder of a holiday for years to come. Imported from abroad, they were printed with either a motto, 'Present From' legend or town crest and intended as a keepsake of a visit, while also promoting the location to others who later admired them back home. Pre-First World War items were usually back-stamped 'Germany' or 'Bohemia', while those stamped 'Foreign' are likely to have originated from Japan.

Receipts can often provide details that you could never hope to find anywhere else. This 1902 cruise receipt is a goldmine of information, giving the name of the couple taking the trip, the date of the voyage, the name of the steamer, the berth occupied and the price paid.

Just as we keep memorabilia from trips we have taken today, our ancestors would have done the same. This can take many forms, including the original posters, fliers and newspaper advertising that would have promoted the trip. This example in a January 1931 edition of the London Charivari advertises a voyage with the Royal Mail Steam Packet Company.

Other indicators of a trip could include a ship's plans, advertising the shipping company and promoting the layout of the vessel, or smaller items collected onboard that are embellished with the shipping logo, such as crested ceramics, spoons and even buttons that may have found their way into your ancestor's luggage.

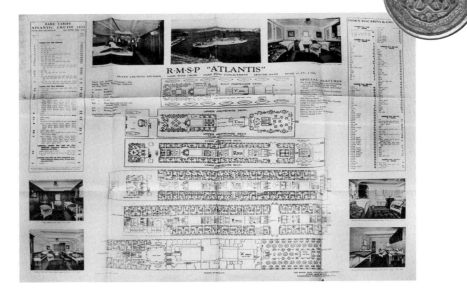

The souvenir industry became a staple trade in seaside resorts providing seasonal jobs for many locals and a vital part of the holiday culture for visitors.

Ask yourself:
* Is there a pattern to the souvenirs that your ancestors collected?
* Do they all come from one particular destination, indicating that this was where they spent regular holidays?
* Could you expand on their collection by seeking out other related souvenirs and period pieces?

Throughout the Victorian era regular fairs were held across Britain. Travelling from village to village, these events enabled locals to attend for the day and provided a fun and carefree change from their otherwise work-orientated lives. Villagers would wear their Sunday best, women would decorate their hair with flowers and enjoy the chance to be feminine, and the children would look forward to spending the few pence they had been given.

As a reminder of the day, it was often possible to purchase small ceramic items – sometimes of a 'cheeky' nature – to display upon their mantelpieces back home. These were aptly named 'fairings'.

Not all holiday souvenirs were ceramic based. Wooden items, known collectively as 'treen', were extremely popular. Named after the location in Ayrshire in which it was originally produced, Mauchline ware was printed with picturesque views from around the country and displayed on a variety of small wooden objects from snuffboxes and small sewing cases to tea caddies and postage-stamp holders. Generally made from sycamore wood, which gives a pleasing golden colour, the ingenious range of items available meant that holidaymakers could bring home a small but useful memento of their trip depicting the place they had visited. Early examples were hand-painted, then from the 1820s transfer-printed designs were used, followed by photographs from the 1860s. A glossy varnish was painted over the top to seal and protect the piece. Another decoration in this range was tartanware. From the mid-1800s, colourful plaid-printed paper was glued to each item before varnish was added; from the 1870s, fernware was popular on boxes and other souvenirs covered with leaf-designed papers or delicate fern-frond stencils. A single example or collection could form the basis of a lasting reminder of your ancestor's travels.

Scotland did not hold the monopoly on wooden souvenirs however, and the Kent spa town of Tunbridge Wells was equally well known for its beautiful boxes. Marquetry techniques were used, adapting the practices carried out in furniture production to develop the 'stickwork' method where narrow canes of different-coloured wood are cut into paper-thin tiles called 'tesserae' and added to the surface of a box in a mosaic pattern. Various other items were embellished in the same way, with craftsmen showing their woodwork skills by the intricacy of the designs produced. Due to the tiny pieces of wood used to create the layout, there is always the chance that some of these pieces may have come away from the main body of the item over years of use. Tunbridge ware is highly desirable today, so check your find for signs of wear: these are treasures where condition defines value.

PRIZED POSTCARDS

We have all come across an old postcard sent by a relative from a holiday destination and kept as a reminder of a special location or purely for the pictorial image, but did you know that the obsession with these mini 'word and picture packages', known as deltiology, is thought to be one of the top three 'collectable' hobbies in the world alongside coin and stamp collecting?

A postcard is a thin piece of rectangular cardboard, usually with an image on one side, intended for writing on and mailing without an envelope. The first commercially produced card was created in 1861 by John P. Charlton of Philadelphia, USA, although it had no image. Léon Besnardeau created an illustrated card at Camp Conlie, a training camp for soldiers of the Franco-Prussian War, but these acted as war memorabilia with images of armaments and military emblems. It wasn't until January 1869 that Dr Emmanual Hermann of Vienna rejuvenated the idea of producing printed postcards and on 1 October 1869 the Austrian Post Office issued the world's first official postcard. Two and a quarter million were sold in the first three months and other countries soon followed suit. Initially known as 'correspondence cards', the British Postmaster General recommended their official production in October 1870. Printed by the firm De La Rue, each card incorporated a stamp with a new postal rate of a half penny, half the rate of letter postage in an envelope, ensuring that the new postcards were an immediate success.

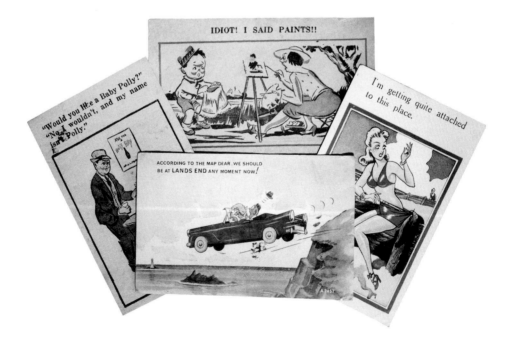

Postcards with cartoon-style images and saucy captions appealed to the sense of humour of the 1930s British holidaymaker when they sent their 'wish you were here' messages home.

The British versions still lacked illustrations and in 1872 private firms were allowed to add pictorial advertising and images as long as they included the prepaid stamp. The real breakthrough in restrictions came in September 1894 when postcards were allowed to be sent with an adhesive stamp, enabling publishers to sell postcards to the public and expand their range of images. Initially these were views of local towns, not photographed but instead created in an engraved line drawing format by professional artists. Photographic postcards began to appear from the 1890s, using lithography and the photogravure printing processes of the day.

Postcard usage gathered momentum at the start of the twentieth century when the Post Office allowed both the correspondence and the address to be written on the same side of the card with a division down the middle, freeing up the opposite side for the image. Along with capturing pictures of royal weddings, Boer War military subjects, famous figures and landmarks, they became the standard method of conveying short messages to friends and loved ones due to their economical postage costs. Later, it was the cartoon-style images embellished with saucy captions that appealed to the outgoing nature of the 1930s holidaymaker. If there was ever a way of understanding your ancestor's opinions on a particular location, the limited space provided on a postcard enabled them to briefly describe their destination and the activities they were taking part in – invaluable evidence of travel. (See also Chapter 4, Postcard Glossary.)

What Next?

Taking a holiday would have been an important part of your ancestor's year, a date to be looked forward to and the memories of it cherished in the months afterwards. Have you inherited any mementoes of their travels? Check through any paper ephemera that you may previously have overlooked for advertising posters, leaflets, tour guides and tickets: all can provide clues as to where their favourite holidays were spent. Dig out old photo albums and seek out seaside shots, study their dress, the scene in the background and perhaps their relaxed appearance. Looking deeper into a photograph may help you to date and pinpoint a specific location or era. Read, read and read again any correspondence they may have left relating to their travel arrangements and destinations.

By talking to your family or reading a diary entry you may discover that one or more of your ancestors travelled abroad by ship. Try and track them down using the site *www.ancestorsonboard.com*, which is a database of outbound passengers from the British Isles between 1890 and 1960. Before the First World War it was not compulsory to travel with a passport. Although records are few and far between, it may be worth trying to track down possible family passport applications, which could provide further clues to your ancestor's movements. Visit *www.nationalarchives.gov.uk* to discover how to start your search.

Whatever their reason – military or missionary, tourist or trailblazer, holiday-maker or new-home dweller – chart your ancestor's movements and illustrate their adventures with period items from railway tickets and timetables to cruise memorabilia and baggage labels, creating a real and lasting testimony to their travels.

THREE

A STAMP OF APPROVAL

Be like a postage stamp. Stick to one thing until you get there.

Josh Billings

Sent in their hundreds of thousands, a letter from the past is a true testament to the thoughts and feelings of the sender and can provide a calendar of events and perhaps tackle subjects recorded in no other location. Looking beyond the content, the style of letter or envelope, the paper it is written on and the type of postal method used can all help to link it to a particular period if you find it to be dateless or the stamp has been removed.

Delivering the country's mail has been a long and complicated journey and the changing rules and regulations help us to understand how our postal system has developed.

Step Back in Time

Poste Haste

The Romans are credited with bringing the first messenger system to Britain and in the centuries that followed, future generations made use of the Roman roads to deliver mail from the sender to the recipient on horseback. As Britain's towns and cities began to grow, trade became an important part of the economy and a good communication system was essential. Specific postal routes were established and coaching inns provided a means of resting the horses and breaking the journey between destinations.

It wasn't long before the system was in disarray when individual carriers began providing their own services. To ensure that all mail was dealt with by the state, a proclamation was enforced in 1609 forbidding unofficial carriers to operate. By 1635, Charles I saw an opportunity to generate revenue and began to make the service available to the general public with the postage being paid by the recipient.

The General Post Office (GPO) was created later, after the Restoration of the monarchy. Under the ruling of Charles II, with Henry Bishop as the first Postmaster General, the GPO became the sole carrier of UK post, establishing organised and effective methods of delivery and creating a handstamp to show when letters had been received in their offices. With control of the Post Office now passing from the king's household to the treasury, all profits went to the state and were regularly used to fund British military campaigns.

As England's capital city, London was chosen to trial a local system designed by William Dockwra, which allowed items weighing up to 1lb to be delivered for one penny. Each piece was stamped with a postmark enabling it to be delivered on the same day that it was received in their offices. Once the validity of the scheme was established and the legalities ironed out, the government officially took over the system in London in 1682. As a result, Penny Posts spread to other towns and cities, offering a single rate of postage in a specified area and calculated by weight, although by 1801, the rate of the London Penny Post had increased to tuppence to help fund the war against Napoleon.

The greatest postal reform got underway from 1839 when Rowland Hill improved the system by creating a Uniform Penny Post. The country moved swiftly from a system based on the number of sheets per letter and the mileage to deliver, to a fixed rate based on weight. In operation from May 1840, the world's first prepaid postage stamp went on sale. Known as the Penny Black, the stamp not only changed the face of mail delivery, but helped provide work for thousands of men and women up and down the country.

MARVELLOUS MULREADYS

Issued in the UK in 1840, at the same time as the release of the Penny Black stamp, were the beautifully decorated Mulready envelopes. Sceptical from the outset, the public were not really used to envelopes, which on the old postal system had counted as an extra sheet of paper and therefore doubled the postal rate. Each prepaid Mulready envelope and letter sheet was issued in both one penny and two pence denominations and although they are highly collectable today they were considered condescending because of their elaborate, whimsical designs and long-winded rules and regulations printed on each letter sheet. Expense was also a consideration when the sender realised that they could still post a folded letter sheet, sealed with wax and with the addition of a new stamp and save the additional cost of the envelope. Rowland Hill had thought the Mulready would be the main vehicle for letters, but they soon fell out of favour as the general public preferred to use the Penny Black stamp to add to their own simple stationery.

Due to their fairly limited lifespan, the discovery of a Mulready in your ancestor's belongings helps you date it to a period in the mid-nineteenth century. Two colours were used to distinguish between the denominations: one-penny envelopes were designed in black ink on cream paper while the two pence version stood out in blue ink on cream paper. Initially, the value was printed at the bottom of the envelope which remained stampless, but as soon as the stamp became the excepted method of paying for postage, a printed stamp was incorporated into the design.

Today, we can appreciate the caricatures and parodies of life interpreted on the Mulready, which were a work of art.

The Mulready was introduced on 6 May 1840 as an envelope and lettersheet. The example shows one penny and two pence Mulready envelopes. The one penny was used from London to Kirkwall, Orkney Islands, on 7 May 1840, and the two pence was used from London to Bristol on 6 August 1840. They are both stamped with a red Maltese cross, cancelling Britannia as per the regulations. (Robin Cassell/Mulready Philatelics/www.mulreadyphilatelics.co.uk)

Key Events

1635 Charles I makes the Royal Mail service available to the general public.

1660 Charles II establishes the General Post Office (GPO) in England.

1680 William Dockwra first introduces the London Penny Post for local deliveries.

1784 John Palmer creates an efficient mail coach delivery service to operate throughout Britain.

1830 An agreement was made with the Liverpool and Manchester Railway and the GPO to transport mail by rail.

1840 On 10 January the Uniform Penny Post is introduced throughout Britain.

1840 In May, the world's first postage stamps are introduced in the form of the Penny Black, thanks to Rowland Hill, and become valid for prepaid postage.

1959 The UK postcode system is established.

What Next?

With every piece of family correspondence you could carry out the following investigations.

Ask yourself:
* What is the relationship between the correspondent and yourself?
* Why did the subject matter warrant a letter? Was it just a means of keeping in touch with a few lines of general chit chat or was it to convey important news?
* Was the letter written from a significant place: America after emigration to a new country, the Western Front during the First World War, or a spa town during recuperation from illness?
* Are other family members mentioned?
* Are any significant events mentioned that could help with dating?
* Consider the type of writing instrument used: quill, metal-tipped ink pen, pencil. Is the paper handmade or mass produced? Is there a watermark of the maker and does the paper quality give a clue to the writer's social standing?
* Has the envelope survived and is the stamp and postal cancellation intact giving you an obvious clue to the date?
* Can you follow up on the address of the recipient or sender? Do the addresses still exist today? Can you arrange to visit them? Do future generations still live or work at the properties? Use genealogy websites, maps and local archive libraries to track down individuals and specific locations.
* Delve deeply into the contents. Trade and commercial dealings can be investigated from the headed notepaper, travel schedules shed light on the transport arrangements of the era and gentle terms of endearment can chart the love affairs of days gone by.

The lost art of handwriting is thanks to our love of the typewriter and, today, the personal computer, but during the Victorian era being able to produce a well-crafted letter was paramount. At this time paper correspondence was used for introductions, apologies, thanks, congratulations and numerous other occasions. Not only the content, but also the appearance of the letter belied a person's social standing. Lack of care, ink blotches and scratching out were frowned upon. Clean, clear and legible copperplate handwriting was expected without the use of foreign phrases or the need for underlining, which in some instances was thought to be vulgar. In the event of a misspelling, the letter needed to be rewritten. The tone should be matched to the recipient, whether tradesperson or intimate friend.

In the 1850s, it was acceptable for women to spritz their letters with perfume and use ribbons or add small sketches for embellishment. Men were expected to correspond on plain paper, perhaps with the addition of a monogram, finished with sealing wax. Even the sealing wax had to be the correct colour: red for business, black for mourning. By 1900, fashions had changed and using wax as a sealant gradually began to fall out of favour.

Every aspect of a piece of correspondence holds a new clue, it is just a matter of studying the item thoroughly.

TELEGRAMS

After the introduction of the prepaid stamp, the next challenge was to 'quench the public's thirst' for faster, more efficient communication over long distances, and by the 1850s this was recognised with the electric telegraph system. Although the process greatly reduced the time it took to deliver the message by postal methods it was considerably more expensive, initially making the service only accessible to governments, military personnel and commercial traders. In 1853, the privately owned English and Irish Magnetic Telegraph Company issued some of the first telegraph stamps, but when this and other telegraph companies were nationalised, the Post Office began to issue telegraph stamps from 1876.

On 24 July 1935, greetings telegrams were introduced in Britain, allowing people to have their telegrams delivered on specially illustrated forms in golden envelopes for the an extra three pence. It gave the chance for telegrams to convey joyous news of happy occasions, with nearly 25,000 being sent in the first week. The designs were beautifully created by artists of the day, including Frank Newbould, Edward Ardizzone and Claudia Freedman. Rex Whistler started a tradition by designing the first Valentine's greetings telegram in 1936 and thereafter they became an annual occurrence every Valentine's Day.

Is it possible that your ancestor sent one of these messages? Can you date your greetings telegram to one of these early examples and what was the important news that your ancestors wished to convey?

In December 1940, during the Second World War, the golden envelopes used to deliver greetings telegrams were changed to white with blue printing to enable the telegram delivery boys to read the addresses more clearly during times of blackout. Gradually, the necessities of war and the shortages suffered meant that the telegrams were printed in a simplified format to save on both paper and ink until in April 1943 the greetings service was suspended altogether.

It was not until the end of paper rationing in November 1950 that greetings telegrams were reintroduced. Designed by Claudia Freedman, they were printed in red and black and delivered in a yellow envelope. Other artists created innovative ideas, including special designs intended for specific events.

The demise of the telegram and subsequent telegraph material began with the increasing popularity of the telephone and, later, the fax machine. Although right up to the third quarter of the twentieth century telegrams were sent to congratulate couples on their wedding day or to announce the birth of a child, they had also become linked as the bearers of bad news due to their use in the two world wars for relaying messages of casualties and fatalities in battle: an association that had been hard to break. Finally, in 1982, British Telecom closed the Inland Telegram service, signalling the end of an era and a method of communication now only experienced by our forebears.

What Next?

For more information about all aspects of the postal system, the procedures and occupations involved, visit The British Postal Museum & Archive at *http://post-alheritage.org.uk*. Its website is packed with features on everything from how mail has been delivered through the ages and the type of services offered to examples of paper-related ephemera, employment records of those within the industry and how methods of communication have developed.

FOUR

READING BETWEEN THE LINES

A moment lasts all of a second, but the memory lives on forever.

Unknown

Military memorabilia has long been an absorbing area for collectors. Battle and regimental keepsakes, weaponry and personal items each have their particular expert band of antiquarian followers, but what can the discovery of such an item tell the family historian?

War and conflict can have a huge impact on a family and, as a result, it is often a few precious items from these periods that stand the test of time. Kept for both remembrance and sentimental reasons, this is an area where the smallest examples can tell a whole story about your ancestor's past. You may have the good fortune to unearth a family letter describing a soldier's life or a particular incident during his or her service within the armed forces or alternatively have come across something as simple as a regimental cap badge. Whatever clue you have been given, your prior research of documentary evidence will help provide access and understanding of the physical items our forebears either left behind or came into contact with. The subject matter is crying out for you to purchase similar items reflecting an individual's career so don't be put off if your shoebox hunting initially seems fruitless. Building a back story is half the fun.

CAP BADGES AND HELMET PLATES

A cap badge distinguishes the wearer's nationality or the organisation to which they belonged. In the British and Commonwealth armies each regiment and corps had its own individual badge and insignia that set it apart from its contemporaries. Originally, these badges were made of brass, but during the Second World War metals were required for alternative use so the cap badges were produced in plastic. This tradition continued from 1950 onwards when Stay-Brite – a plastic that is economical to produce and low maintenance – replaced the brass and white metal badges.

Some regiments preferred to use other terms to describe these badges. The Coldstream Guards called theirs the 'Capstar'; the Queen's Lancashire Regiment favoured the name 'Motto' while the Royal Horse Artillery christened theirs a 'Cypher'. Bear in mind that sometimes a badge was worn with additional decoration to reflect a regiment's historical activities. For example, it is often traditional for Scottish regiments to wear their badge on a small piece of regimental tartan, while officer cadets may wear theirs showcased on a small piece of white backing. Hackles, or feather plumes, could be incorporated behind the badge and were especially popular with Scottish and Irish fusilier regiments.

Did You Know?

In the British Army, depending upon the type of headdress, the cap badge is positioned differently.

* On the beret, the badge is positioned approximately 1in above the left eye.
* On a dress cap, the badge is positioned centrally, above the eyebrows.
* On a feather bonnet and fusilier cap, the badge is on the cap between the left ear and eye (closer to the ear).
* On the Scottish tam o'shanter, the glengarry and the side cap, the position of the badge is in between the left eye and left ear.

Use this knowledge when trying to identify and understand more about dress codes in your military photographs.

What Next?

There are some fantastic websites and specialist dealers who can help you in your quest to locate a particular badge, button or buckle and they are usually only too happy to tell you about your own items in a little more detail. They can point you in the direction of complementary pieces that you should look out for, explain their meanings and significance, and even help you to date not only your item but perhaps even an old photograph featuring your ancestor in military uniform. Sometimes the smallest piece of memorabilia can form the entry point into your ancestor's military past. The website *www.kellybadge.co.uk* has images of over 5,400 badges and buttons, ranging from military rank badges to civil police patches and insignia.

Not all badges have military connections, so look out for long-service awards, occupational commendations and membership or society emblems.

The Royal Army Service Corps was responsible for land, coastal and lake transport, air despatch and the supply of food, water, fuel and general domestic stores. Could the discovery of a badge or medal tell you more about your ancestor's activities? (Stewart Coxon)

MILITARY MEDALS

As the British Empire flourished and expanded, medals were often issued to celebrate successes, but those of most importance were the ones issued for bravery, either individually or as part of a combined effort. The first campaign medal given to every soldier regardless of his rank was the 1815 Waterloo Medal. Highly prized, this medal was engraved on the rim with the recipient's name and the regiment in which they served. By 1856, the gallantry medal known as the Victoria Cross was also attainable by all ranks.

Alongside handwritten letters, the discovery of a medal can be extremely emotional, especially if you then take on the challenge of finding out why it was awarded and the regiment and campaigns in which the recipient was involved. The need to find out about their military career can become addictive and your discoveries can often answer questions about the personality and character of the individual and their outlook on life.

Examine your medal and do your research. Some examples will have been issued with bars across them that have been stamped with the relevant battles and the dates on which they were fought. Others include the 1914 Star, the British War Medal and the Victory Medal, issued in huge numbers to those men who took part in the First World War. Similar medal groupings were given during the Second World War and casualty medals were issued posthumously.

Your ancestor may have taken part in other campaigns such as the Crimean War, the Indian Mutiny of 1857 or even the Zulu Wars of 1877–9. Although you would be unlikely to want to part with the medals awarded, they can now command a high price among collectors so it is worth getting a valuation from an expert if only for insurance purposes.

Top Tip

For Preservation and Protection

If you do not intend to display your medals, and to ensure that corrosion of the metal does not take place, store them in protective acid-free tissue paper.

If a medal is in good condition but the ribbons look worn and perhaps a little dirty, turn the ribbon inside out to expose the fresh, clean side to give the award a new lease of life. If the ribbon is beyond saving, consider having it professionally replaced.

Regiments wore their medals 'court' or 'royal' style, which means they were placed side-by-side with stiffened ribbons behind; or hanging freely in what was known as a 'swing' or 'standard' style. If you wish to display your medals in a case or deep-mounted frame, try to find out how your ancestor's regiment wore its medals and showcase them accordingly.

However you decide to present these awards, always try to keep them out of direct sunlight to ensure that the ribbons do not fade.

CONFLICT AND COMBAT

From the beginning of the Victorian era to the end of the Second World War, there were a number of conflicts in which your family may have taken part or experienced the repercussions of. Are there any individuals missing from certain census years who you cannot account for? If so, perhaps they were away serving their country. The most obvious hostilities are the two world wars, but also consider the other battles that they may have encountered.

American Civil War

Fought between April 1861 and 1865, the American Civil War took place between the northern and southern states.

As a nation, Britain never entered the war and was officially neutral, but a large number of individuals served on both sides, with most in the Confederate Army. Their military experience made them stand out from the crowd and often resulted in swift promotion through the ranks to lead a unit. Although the majority of those on the Confederate side were undocumented, sixty-seven Britons in the Union Army won Congressional Medals of Honour.

Have you inherited military memorabilia from this period, regimental records or even a bundle of letters written home to a loved one?

Did You Know?

Perhaps you've heard a family story that your ancestor 'contributed' towards the civil war effort but never actually left the shores of Britain. If this has left you confused, then delve deeper into the individual's occupation.

Liverpool handled the majority of the cotton trade from the southern (Confederate) states to supply the mills in Lancashire and felt the full effect of the conflict when the northern states began to block the passage of Confederate ships. Naturally, the city's allegiance fell with its trading partners.

In 1862, the John Laird Sons and Company dockyard near Birkenhead built two ships for the Confederate side in secret, the most famous of these being the CSS *Alabama*. The docks on the River Mersey are now the only American Civil War site of historical importance outside the United States.

It is also said that the last gunshot of the battle was fired from a weapon crafted in Liverpool's Duke Street.

Ask yourself:

* Could your ancestor have been employed in these shipbuilding or gunsmith trades at the time of the American Civil War?
* Have you any pieces of family memorabilia, letters or journal entries that refer to this period in history and had you previously failed to make the link? These are often discoveries that you only make when you re-examine your family ephemera in greater depth and begin to slowly fit the random jigsaw pieces together.

★ Have you inherited any newspaper cuttings, occupational information and trade journals that could help confirm dates of employment and even involvement? Re-question relatives, making specific lines of enquiry–and who knows what connected items could be lying around waiting to be discovered.

First and Second World Wars

When war was declared on 4 August 1914, many people joined up to show their support in the mistaken belief that the troubles would be over by Christmas. Posters encouraged volunteers to enlist, the most famous one being Lord Kitchener pointing at the viewer with the caption 'Your country needs you'. Others played more on the emotions with scenes of the womenfolk encouraging their men to go to war. After an initial request for 100,000 men, a second call was announced for 500,000 more. By 1916, 3 million men had volunteered, but it still wasn't enough after the massive losses sustained.

On 2 March 1916 conscription was introduced, specifying that single men between the ages of 18 and 41 would be called up for military service. This was later extended to include married men and men up to the age of 51. These rapid changes in the law show just how desperate the country was to add new men to support the campaign. Those men who refused to fight were known as conscientious objectors. Many of them were pacifists who believed it was wrong to kill another human being. Some agreed to perform non-combat duties and worked in weapons factories or went to the front line to become stretcher bearers to aid the wounded. Those known as absolutists refused to perform any form of service and were totally opposed to war; there was little compassion for their cause among local communities and they were often treated harshly or stigmatised for their beliefs.

Women's Voluntary Service (WVS) Civil Defence badge. Although full uniforms may not have survived, cloth and metal badges may have been removed and kept as mementoes of their service. (Home Front Museum)

CRITICAL COMMUNICATIONS

The First World War saw serious messages and images find their way onto postcards, as patriotic and propaganda subjects became a popular way to show off events and the changing way of life at this time. Writing letters home became a vital link for soldiers and service postcards were issued to the troops on the front line, but censorship remained strict. Zeppelins, warships and military themes were popular, along with thought-provoking illustrations of wives and mothers thinking about their loved ones away at the front line. The latter were often accompanied by a short verse or sentiment.

Silk-embroidered postcards were first made for the Paris Exposition in 1900 and they came into their own during the First World War. Painstakingly embroidered patterns were hand sewn onto strips of silk mesh by French and Belgian women, taking between 4 and 8 hours per image to complete. These strips were then sent to be cut into sections and mounted onto postcards. Later, these techniques were improved with sewing machines in a factory environment and the results meant that they became a popular keepsake for soldiers as a reminder of their war service, or as a love token or simple upbeat greeting that could be sent home to their families to avoid touching upon the harsh realities of the conflict. It is thought that as many as 10 million cards were produced between 1914 and 1919.

A wide range of subjects were used for decoration, from hearts and flowers to birds, patriotic flags and regimental emblems, with various greetings added depending upon the time of year. There are two main formats in which this type of postcard was created: either in a panel version with the embroidery fixed to the front of the card or an envelope design created from the silk with space for a small card inside.

The Second World War saw a resurgence in this type of postcard, but those produced were machine made and simpler in design and they never quite gained the popularity of their First World War predecessors.

For the family historian the postcard is an essential resource. Not only might you discover more about family movement and travel by following the address trail of the recipient but you may also uncover a handwriting sample of an ancestor. Clothing styles, the transport used and the streets where your forebears lived may all be depicted on the postcards of the era. When stamps have been removed, the handstamp and accompanying date can often disappear with it, making it difficult to date when the correspondence was sent. Learn how to identify the types of postcards produced in order to narrow down a time frame and tie the sender and recipient's details to a particular ancestor.

Postcard Glossary

appliqué: A technique whereby fabric, feathers, real hair and other materials were added to a postcard to create texture. As a result, they were often heavier and cost the sender more to post.

First World War embroidered postcards and silk keepsakes, mementoes from a time of conflict kept to remember a loved one or as a souvenir of their involvement. (Bottom image: Stewart Coxon)

bas–relief: A raised surface that is often quite pronounced to accentuate areas such as dresses, faces and hair on an image. This was a patented process and more defined than straightforward embossing.

court card: 4½ x 3½in-sized cards that were privately produced in Britain between 1894 and 1899 and were limited in size by the postal authorities.

mechanical postcards: These had moving parts: rotating wheels to include additional data or flaps to reveal further images or a novelty design.

real photo postcards: Real photographic prints were developed onto a piece of card with postcard markings on the back. They were of much higher quality and the image had better definition than an image of photographic origin created in large numbers via a printing process.

topo postcards: Topographical cards displayed images of landmarks, towns, villages and buildings, making them excellent geographical resources for the family historian as not only do those that have been sent contain a message from the recipient, but the image also shows a particular area of the world at a certain point in history. Local scenes are a fabulous way of seeing just how a location has changed over the decades.

undivided back postcards: These carried the recipient's address and postage stamp on one side and a message written in a space on the other side alongside the image. In 1902, the divided back appeared where the image stood alone on the front and the back was divided into an area to write the recipient's details along with an area for the message.

vignettes: The image was printed in such a way that the colour tone faded to blend in with the white space around it. This was ideal for undivided backed postcards, allowing slightly more space for the sender to write their message.

write away postcards: Produced with the first few words of a message already incorporated in the design, i.e. 'You'll hardly believe'. The sender would then continue with their own message. These were popular in the early 1900s.

MEDIA COVERAGE

Newspapers and magazines published wartime events as they unfolded. Any of these publications that have survived can help you to comprehend how rapidly the war progressed.

The lack of television meant that radio was important to convey messages. It was supported by a whole host of posters that conveyed the requests of the government and related war ministries: women were called on to train for a variety of jobs, with the slogan 'A woman must fill a man's place', while food shortages saw posters appear that encouraged people to 'Do your bit – save food'.

Perhaps you've discovered newspaper clippings or even a poster or wartime propaganda among your ancestor's possessions. Ask yourself what was going through their minds at the time as you try to understand your ancestors a little better.

Consider *why* they kept such ephemera, their feelings and emotions. Perhaps:

* They felt strongly about the subject advertised.
* They wanted to play their part in whatever role necessary.
* They wanted to provide support from the home front, feed their families and maintain a home for their loved ones to come back to.
* They wanted to volunteer for work on the land or in factories.
* They wanted to raise money for wartime funds.

MORALE-BOOSTING MEMORABILIA

Christmas was a desperate time during the war years. To lift military spirits, a gift was given to the troops to recognise their services. Queen Victoria started the tradition during the Boer War with a tin of chocolates for each of her troops. Princess Mary followed the tradition during the Second World War with a brass-embossed tin containing a variety of items from chocolates and cigarettes to acid tablets and a khaki writing case. The contents depended upon whether the recipient was a smoker or not, and the dietary and religious requirements of the Indian troops were also taken into account. Nurses in the front-line field hospitals were also issued with these festive tokens and by the third Christmas at war the sick and wounded in hospital or in clearing stations were included in the gift giving.

This was a mammoth task for all concerned, from production to distribution. The Imperial War Museum website has a detailed article, illustrated with images, on the procedure, which is well worth a read. Many recipients kept the gift boxes as a reminder of their wartime contributions and these have been passed down within families. Perhaps you've discovered such an item in your ancestor's belongings and until now did not realise its significance. Find out more by visiting the Imperial War Museum collections at *www.iwm.org.uk/collections/search*.

Advertising used to encourage volunteers to join the Women's Land Army. (Home Front Museum)

What of Jack Tar this Christmas Time?

Send Him a Daily Sketch Christmas Tin.

YOU would not like to spend your Christmas in the same circumstances and conditions as our gallant handy-men, away from wife and children, relations, and friends. No cheery Christmas fare—no happy party—no warm and glowing fire, but the cold, cold wind far out on the ocean, manning Dreadnought, destroyer, and submarine.

Think how our Jack Tars will long for home and the comforts of their family circles. Spare a thought for those who will keep up a constant vigil, guarding our shores and making Christmas and home life possible.

Surely of all men Jack has earned his Christmas Box. Then send him the best—a *Daily Sketch* Christmas Tin. You could not make a better purchase—you could not send Jack a more acceptable gift.

Remember that by the splendidly generous co-operation of the under-mentioned well-known Firms nearly 10/- worth of goods is contained in each 5/- *Daily Sketch* Tin.

When Jack opens his tin he will find goods that could not be better chosen—delicious milk chocolate that will help to sustain him—warmth-giving peppermints that will comfort him on deck beside his guns—a fine briar pipe and tobacco and plenty of cigarettes.

How his heart will rejoice, and his thoughts will go out to you who has remembered him and his Christmas Day. Let him say to his mates, "Old England has not forgotten us."

5/- will send a Jack Tar a Daily Sketch Christmas Tin Containing :—

A 6-oz. Tin of English Peppermint,
Supplied by Messrs. A. J. Caley and Son, Ltd., Norwich.

¼-lb. of "Oceanic" Navy Cut Tobacco,
Supplied by Messrs. R. and J. Hill, Ltd., London.

A "Berik" high-class Briar Pipe,
Supplied by Messrs. Tennant and Son, Ltd., Berwick-on-Tweed.

100 "Chairman" Virginian Cigarettes,
Supplied by Messrs. R. J. Lea, Ltd., Manchester.

¼-lb. Best Quality Milk Chocolate,
Supplied by Messrs. J. S. Fry and Sons, Ltd., Bristol, and Messrs. A. J. Caley and Son, Ltd., Norwich.

The *Daily Sketch* has undertaken the enormous task of packing and delivering the Tins to the Admiralty depot, and it is absolutely essential to avoid delay.

During the First World War, the Princess Mary commemorative tin was sent out to those involved in the conflict to lift spirits at Christmas. Could you have inherited one of these mementoes?

AMERICA REMEMBERS THE CHILDREN.

It will be a tragic Christmas in many, many homes. This little dolly is one of the 10,000,000 gifts being sent from America to the countries at war.—(Underwood.)

Advertisements were placed in newspapers during the First World War to encourage people at home to purchase a Christmas box to be sent to serving naval men. This Daily Sketch *advertisement from 1914 details just what would have been included for our naval ancestors. Newspaper cuttings provide a valuable insight into life at specific points in history.*

The array of items that have survived the most desperate conditions of war is surprising. Some pieces show signs of wear and tear and are slightly 'battle weary', others look as pristine as the day they were made. Notebooks, plans, maps, training manuals and pamphlets form just some of the paper ephemera alongside personal diaries, censored letters, patriotic pledge cards, medical reports and recruitment cards. You may come across personal items such as webbing, belts, holsters, wash rolls, razors and combs from their kit bags, which have been lovingly kept by ex-service personnel as a reminder of a time when they served their country with pride.

From Boer War swagger sticks and Second World War silk escape maps to gas masks and Women's Land Army insignia, the website World War Wonders will help you to identify your pieces, enable you to date them and start you on your road to further research. With hundreds of examples for sale you may even feel inspired to start a military collection yourself. Find out more at *www.worldwarwonders.co.uk*.

The end of both world wars saw a flurry of memorabilia produced. Most popular were the mugs that marked Victory Day. The word 'Peace' or a symbolic dove featured among images of flags of the Allied nations and their military and political leaders. Victory Day was celebrated in the streets across the country, work was abandoned and church bells rang out to celebrate the end of the conflicts. Did your ancestor keep any memorabilia from this time?

Don't be surprised if you find yourself wanting to learn more about the conflicts in which your ancestors were involved. There are numerous historical resources online for you to visit, just type your interests into *www.google.co.uk* and follow the trail. Why not consider reading the personal recollections of those involved? Diaries and letters have been transcribed online of those who were 'actually there' and make compelling reading for anyone with a connection. A war nurse's diary describing her work in a Belgian field hospital during the First World War could mirror your own ancestor's career, see *http://net.lib.byu.edu/~rdh7/wwi/memoir/warnurse/wnTC.html*. The recollections of trench survivors, wireless operators and wartime captives can all be found at *http://www.firstworldwar.com/diaries/index.htm*.

FIVE

REGULATIONS AND RESTRICTIONS

Learn from yesterday, live for today, hope for tomorrow.

Anonymous

Of course, not all of our ancestors were involved in military action during the wars, but many hundreds of thousands experienced the difficulties and dilemmas indirectly on the home front. Their memories and mementoes from this period of history provide essential clues about what life during shortages, rationing and the constant threat of tragic news from the front line was really like.

We've probably all heard of the ration books and national identity cards that were in use during and shortly after the Second World War, but understanding why they were introduced and what impact they had can help us to appreciate the restrictions they imposed on the simplest of tasks.

THE REALITY

With the outbreak of the Second World War in 1939, the startling fact emerged that Britain grew only enough food to feed one person in every three and the majority of products were traded from overseas countries. As an island nation surrounded by the threat of German invasion, shipments of these products were severely limited when the enemy stopped supplies getting through.

Britain's manpower and production skills were diverted into trades that would aid the war effort and gradually consumer items that had once been plentiful became increasingly scarce.

Drastic measures had to be taken to avoid starvation, and to allow everyone a fair share of the basic essentials available, a rationing and points system was introduced. On 29 September 1939, a national register was set up. Identity cards were distributed and the following year ration books and coupons were issued that gave everyone the opportunity to buy products that were restricted. Adjustments were made to the allowances of women who were pregnant; those with small children or others with special needs. To allow the scheme to work, prices had to be controlled. Stamp-like in appearance,

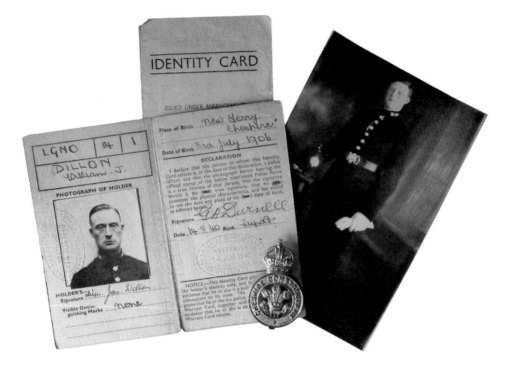

Identity card, photograph and badge belonging to the author's grandfather, a police officer. Have you inherited items that give clues as to your ancestor's occupational past?

the coupons were issued in a variety of colours for everything from fashion and fuel to sweets and sundries. Each book tells a story of the person who owned it.

Did You Know?

If you've come across your forebear's ration book and accompanying identity card it is possible to piece together a picture of a number of years that are not yet accessible via the census. From the information recorded on the national identity card you can discover a person's name, including any middle names, their address at the time of issue and even their signature in their own hand. Most importantly, you will find a passport-sized photograph of the individual, date stamped across the corner by the Foreign Office, and the name of a sponsor to certify that the person in the photograph was who they said they were.

IN SHORT SUPPLY

Generally, the females in our families had the task of creating meals out of the limited supplies they could obtain with their ration coupons, coining the phrase 'making something out of nothing'. Although the system was well thought out and the rations were small, the ingredients meant that the country had a balanced diet with enough vitamins and nutrients to keep them healthy. Butter, sugar, bacon and meat were rationed in early 1940 and by the end of the war virtually half Britain's food was rationed.

Queuing for products became an everyday occurrence with even non-rationed items sometimes being in short supply. Supermarkets as we know them today didn't exist in the 1940s, so to carry out the weekly shop people had to visit individual grocers, butchers and bakers to buy the items on their list. Customers built up a good relationship with the shopkeepers by being loyal to one particular retailer in the hope that a little extra food might be added to their shopping bags.

The shopping routine was particularly hard for those in London and other large cities. Bombing raids constantly threatened the destruction of buildings and shops, further restricting the number of outlets available or delaying essential supplies getting through. A sudden delivery of new products could result in queues around the block as women rushed to buy food to make a simple meal.

Many saved their coupons to get enough lard to make pastry or to buy special items for celebrations. The lack of variety led to 'treats' being sought out from other sources and inevitably a black market emerged where people could get hold of essential or luxury items without using their coupons.

What Next?

Most of us tend to consider the war years as a time for researching the military careers of our ancestors – which, of course, are fascinating and often well docu-mented – but why not give yourself the task of researching the challenges faced by those at home and create an archive of memorabilia to depict that? Ask your older living relatives what they can remember and begin to think what types of ephemera would illustrate their recollections.

As with any restriction, it is human nature to find a way around it and rationing was no different. In the country people were used to growing their own fruit and vegetables which helped to supplement their meagre rations. The Ministry of Agriculture jumped on this idea by introducing its Dig for Victory campaign to encourage the growing of produce on any available land. Allotments sprouted up on parkland, alongside railway lines and even tennis courts and bowling greens were utilised to help provide food for the nation. For those with small gardens, chickens, geese and rabbits were kept to supplement their diets and were fed on scraps, while others joined pig clubs to share the meat when a pig was slaughtered.

Posters and literature still exist that advertised the Dig for Victory cam-paign and your forebears may have made the most of their gardens to put extra food on the table. Then again, your elderly relatives may recall their mother inventing unusual dishes in the kitchen, combining foods that didn't always necessarily go together.

The Ministry of Food had been established by 1940. In overall charge was Lord Woolton who spoke regularly on the radio about what foods were good for you and helped set up a radio programme called *The Kitchen Front,* which offered hints, tips and recipes to housewives. Posters and propaganda gave out the latest information and helped people find alternative ways of making ends meet. Similar helpful facts appeared in the national newspapers along with ready reckoners that could help people work out how to get the most from their rations. Seek out this paper memorabilia at ephemera fairs, search online for specialist sellers or acquire newspaper article copies from the British Newspaper Archive at *http://newspapers.bl.uk/blcs.* Don't forget to read those recipe books that have been handed down through the generations: you may even find your ancestor's favourite recipes and cooking instructions written in their own hand or comments added in the margins.

Visit museums that feature aspects of home front living to get a real feel for the period and to inspire your own collecting possibilities. An excellent example of a dedicated museum is The Home Front Experience in North Wales (New Street, Llandudno LL30 2YF; tel: 01492 871032; website: *www.homefront-museum.co.uk*). With a genuine wartime atmosphere combining the sights and sounds of civilian life, it enables those who lived through it to wallow in nostalgic memories and provides younger generations with the ultimate trip back in time to learn about an era that encouraged community spirit, creativity and a determination to overcome all obstacles.

FASCINATING FACTS

We all pick up sayings or phrases that have been passed down through the family, but have you heard of these, relating especially to the home front period of the 1940s? 'The sight of potato peelings, hurts Lord Woolton's feelings' became a popular catchphrase to discourage waste and promote unconventional uses for even the simplest of things. 'The 4th year of war and you're asked to eat more' was a slogan used to encourage people to eat more vegetables and home-grown produce.

Don't be mistaken into thinking that only food was rationed. The government also imposed clothing controls and the forfeiting of fuel. Clothing coupons were introduced in June 1941 when it became obvious that production costs were too high to be sustained and the factory space could be put to better use for armament and munitions manufacture. The 'Clothing Book' was issued by the Board of Trade and stated firmly on the front cover 'It is your only means of buying clothing'. Inside it explained that 'you must hand the book to the shopkeeper and let him cut the coupons out. It is illegal for the shopkeeper to accept loose coupons'.

Selection of ration books. The details of the book's owner would be filled in on the front; the name and address of the retailer used would be listed inside.

The coupons were produced in pages of different colours from yellow and crimson to magenta and olive to stop people from using them all at once. The government would announce on the radio when they were allowed to start a new colour.

'My father would listen out for different announcements on the radio, discuss the new information with my mother and then she would go and collect the new ration books or register with specific shops,' said Marjorie Martin, who was a young child during the Second World War. 'Children were given a slightly different Clothing Book to their parents, providing extra coupons to allow for them growing out of their clothes during the year.'

Each adult was given a book of sixty-six coupons (later reduced to forty-eight) which was enough to buy them one full set of clothes for the year. These restrictions coined the phrase 'make do and mend': when clothing was worn out people were encouraged to use the material to make something else.

Fuel shortages were an ongoing problem both during and after the war. In 1939, petrol rationing allowed approximately 200 miles of travel per month for each car and by 1942 fuel supplies were cut altogether for private motorists and priority was given to licensed users only, in various classes of vehicle.

If you're trying to track down fuel ration books to add to your collection then examples issued during the war years can be slightly more difficult to come across due to the fact that not everyone had a car. Many of the books date from the 1950s when the Suez Crisis was taking place, so where possible check the dates that the coupons were issued. If in doubt, look at the size of the crown above the ministry logo – a smaller version was published when Queen Elizabeth II came to the throne in 1952 after the death of her father, helping to date post-war examples.

N.B. Fuel ration coupons introduced in 1956 during the Suez Crisis and again in the 1973 Oil Crisis are worth looking out for if you want to bring your collection towards the end of the twentieth century.

RATIONING TIMELINE

June 1941	The distribution of eggs was controlled.
August 1941	Extra cheese ration for manual workers was introduced.
December 1941	Points scheme for food was created allowing the ration book holder to buy from whichever shop they chose.
1941	National dried milk was introduced that could be made up into 4 pints of liquid milk and had to last a family for one month.
April 1942	Lord Woolton launched the National Loaf made from grey, wholemeal flour due to the lack of white flour – it was not popular.
June 1942	American dried egg powder went on sale: one packet was equivalent to a dozen eggs.
July 1942	Sweets were rationed.
December 1944	Extra tea allowance for 70-year-olds and over.

Look out for old newspaper adverts that announced these changes.

THE WOMEN'S LAND ARMY

During both the First and Second World Wars, women were called upon to work in the agricultural roles that their menfolk had been forced to leave when they joined up to fight for their country. Volunteers were requested during the 1914–18 conflict with recruitment posters encouraging women to 'do their bit'. When the government officially recognised the Women's Land Army in 1939, the volunteers were later supplemented with a compulsory call-up to enable food production to sustain those at home. The work these women carried out was indispensable and they continued to support the country long after the war had finished. The Women's Land Army (WLA) finally disbanded in 1950. Did any of your female ancestors have the gritty determination to become a Land Girl? Seek out old family photos showing them in their uniforms of corduroy jodhpurs, green v-necked jumpers and brown hats. The material emblems that were stitched onto their clothing may also have survived.

A National Registration Bill was introduced on 5 September 1939, two days after the declaration of war. National identity cards were issued to aid the control and efficiency of the wartime economy and in preparation for the introduction of rationing. Has a member of your family kept their identity card as a reminder of this period in history? (Top image; author's collection; bottom image: Home Front Museum)

AIR RAID WARDENS

Air raid precautions were introduced to protect people in their homes in the event of attack. Wardens were voluntarily employed to enforce the rules to keep the public safe. They would patrol the streets during blackout to ensure that no light was visible that could alert the enemy, and they would sound the sirens in the event of an air raid before directing people to the purpose-built air raid shelters for protection. A second siren would sound when it was safe to leave. With one in ten bombs dropped on Britain not exploding, the ARP role included evacuating houses, roads and surrounding areas so that these volatile devices could be dealt with or the emergency and rescue services summoned when needed. Their helmets had a large white 'W' stencilled on the front and one may have been passed down in your family if your ancestor had taken on this role. ARP forms were used to assess damage during a raid and for writing a description and location study of the incident. Look out for these types of documents as well as canvas respirator bags, gas masks, and ARP guides to first aid, fire prevention and air attacks.

THE HOME GUARD

Originally known as the Local Defence Volunteers, the Home Guard was a body of men that defended the thousands of miles of British coastline in the event of a German invasion. Consisting of men who were not already part of the regular army due to their reserved occupations or age, they were given military-style training and eventually their own uniforms, as well as weapons, which were often donated by the general public. They would defend key targets such as munitions factories, explosives stores and any open areas where the enemy might invade. Paper ephemera you may come across could include recruitment flyers, training booklets, guidelines from the Home Office and Home Guard rule books, giving a real insight into this essential arm of the home front defences.

Remember

* Always buy the best examples that your pocket will allow. Where possible check for unnecessary tears and creasing to paper memorabilia and try to acquire a selection of complete and used ration coupons to display the comparisons in your albums.
* Store items in archival folders that are acid and lignum free, and keep out of direct sunlight and away from damp conditions that can result in the coupons smelling musty.
* Include relevant newspaper cuttings and ephemera to enhance your collection. Consider other postal stationery from the era, paper currency and postcard imagery to bring the home front experience to life.
* Be aware of copies and reproductions that are now available in packs for educational purposes and can sometimes be mistaken for originals.
* Collecting memorabilia from the home front era can easily be expanded to included product advertising and packaging (see Chapter 8).

SIX

SETTING THE SCENE

Do not remove the ancient landmark that your ancestors set up.
Bible: Hebrew, Proverbs 22:28

Today, many of us rely on satellite navigation to help us find our way on long journeys, but for our ancestors the invention of the map helped to change their lives and charted the highways and byways of Britain and beyond. Whatever the era, the discovery of a map among personal possessions can help to add a new perspective to the individual's life. From simple school sketches of favourite walks and play areas to maps of holiday hotspots, the local village or even a series of illustrations showing industrial changes to a once rural landscape, each map can help us to plot, plan and chart our forebears' movements during a particular stage in their lives.

CHARTING HISTORY

By understanding a little more about the history of map-making we can begin to track down specific examples and date those that we find. If we collect a selection of maps detailing a village, town or region over a succession of years or decades we can work out the changes that occurred and the impact that development and progress had on the lives of residents.

The study and practice of making maps is known as cartography and those employed within the trade are called cartographers. Originally, the North Star was used as a point of reference for early map-makers and explorers as a way of navigating north and determining their point of latitude. The ancient Egyptians and Romans created charts to help delineate boundaries of empires, relying upon the visual information gathered by individuals with knowledge of specific regions that could then be adapted by scholars and hand drawn onto flat maps.

It is thought that Britain was first mapped in AD 150 by Claudius Ptolemaeus, or Ptolemy, a mathematician and geographer from Alexandria. His primitive map listed various tribes, the coordinates of their settlements and information about the major towns. These techniques were expanded upon and by the eleventh century, to aid administration purposes, Britain divided areas of a shire (a traditional term for a division of land) into districts known as 'hundreds', which were mapped out to show the borders and the encompassing towns and villages. In Yorkshire these hundreds were known as 'wapentakes' and in the Kent regions they were called 'lathes'.

To ensure that cartographers were able to sell more than one of their maps, copies had to be produced. Creating duplicates by hand was a long and laborious job. The introduction of the printing process helped make the maps more accessible to the masses and gradually lowered the cost of production. Using a variety of printing methods, which began in twelfth-century China and were followed by Europe in the fifteenth century, 'impressions' started to be made.

N.B. The term 'impression' also referred to the quality of the print and whether the procedure had created a good, clear 'impression' on the page.

A DAUNTING TASK

While many cartographers had to rely on the landscape information provided in journals or second-hand accounts of explorers and adventurers, some had no option but to set themselves the challenge of walking the routes and the often inaccessible areas they planned to chart. They would use their extensive interest in history and excellent mathematical and organisational skills to make notes, take measurements and hand-draw geographical areas to show natural and constructed features, boundaries and important places of interest. Compasses, plotting devices and astronomical instruments were employed and readings were taken from sundials in different locations to help record the contours of the land.

When collecting early examples, it is worth remembering that initially many maps were not drawn to scale and it was often left to the cartographer's discretion to use his artistic licence and imagination. Symbols and other icons were used to record additional geographical information from the difference in continents to the changing of the seasons. As countries and regions were discovered it reduced the need for speculation and, where previously mythical or Biblical characters, plants and animals had been drawn to represent *terra incognita* (Latin for 'unknown lands'), these areas could now be replaced with details of the latest uncharted territories. Many hours were spent, often in poor lighting, outlining the results on vellum, parchment and various other grades of paper.

From bird's-eye views and strip maps to accordion books and detailed scrolls, there was pressure on the cartographer to illustrate maps in new and improved formats. One of the most important changes in the way in which the world was viewed dates back to the sixteenth century. The Dutch cartographer and cosmographer Gerardus Mercator (1512–94) is credited with inventing a machine known as the Mercator Projection, which allowed him to accurately project the spherical world onto a flat piece of paper. As a result, a variety of maps could be created and then bound together in book format. It is one of these volumes that he called an atlas, allowing the growing world to be seen at the turn of a page.

CREATIVELY COLOURED

Understanding more about the colouring methods, symbolism, paper quality and production techniques can all help when it comes to dating or proving the authenticity of a vintage map. When in doubt always consult an expert with your queries, but even the smallest amount of general knowledge on the subject can go a long way in familiarising yourself with the document you have found.

Although Leonardo da Vinci is thought to have been the first to add colour to the contours and elevations of his map of northern Italy, by the sixteenth century the majority of maps were still printed in black and white. Gradually, it was realised that the addition of colour in the form of hand-applied watercolours was found to make them more attractive to the buyer and increase sales.

The seventeenth century saw publishers take advantage of this and the more elaborately decorated the maps became, the better. Specialist artists were employed who

Topographical postcards provide snapshots of local areas and landmarks, which are essential for comparing what a location was like during a particular era and how it might have changed.

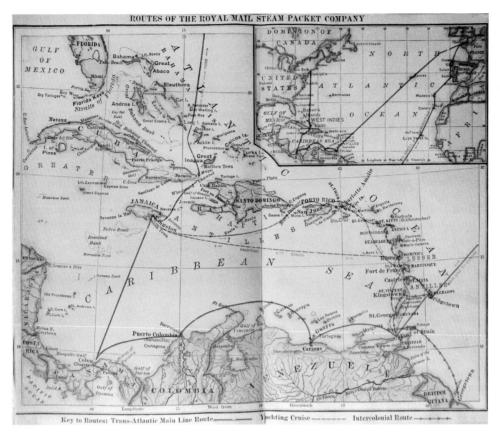

ROUTES OF THE ROYAL MAIL STEAM PACKET COMPANY

Maps are essential for pinpointing locations and may provide details of destinations visited and trips taken.

provided visual appeal by adding green colouring to the parks and woodlands, blues to the rivers, lakes and seas and reds to the towns and cities. Intricate cartouches enclosed important details and heraldic symbols gave an official stamp to each work of art.

The introduction of aquatinting helped to create a more delicate range of tones compared to traditional counterparts. The aquatint etching method was developed in France in the 1600s and Englishman Paul Sandby later perfected a technique that, by adding acid and powdered resin to the printing plates, could recreate the appearance of a watercolour.

Copper engravings allowed the maps to be incised onto a plate using a graver or burin. The image was applied in reverse before ink was added to the surface and then wiped clean so that the ink only remained in the incised grooves. When pressure was added to the plate using a press, the image would transfer onto the paper. Copper is quite a soft metal and it didn't take long for the plates to wear out and the engraved images to become less defined. The introduction of steel plates made a huge difference to this type of printing, not only in the longevity of the plate, but also in the ability to engrave much finer lines and achieve greater detail within the map.

Remember

Compare maps from different periods and note the precision and quality of the printing. Make a list of the features that each example reveals, jot down unusual spellings of locations and look out for period landmarks.

CHANGING TIMES

Ultimately, the focus moved from creating highly embellished works of art to concentrating on providing technically accurate guides for the public. In Britain, the Industrial Revolution of the eighteenth and nineteenth centuries saw the growth of many towns and cities: infrastructure and transport systems changed rapidly, creating new jobs and challenges for budding cartographers who struggled to keep up to date with the latest developments. Civil authorities required detailed maps of the landscape and populated urban areas, placing further demand on the skills of the map-maker, which saw an increase in the amount of newly formed cartography societies that helped to establish the map-maker's art as a specialist profession.

The development of the camera improved their task by allowing them to create a photographic record of particular locations and topographical information, but there was nothing quite like using the hands-on approach to collecting data. Water towers provided good observation points and even hot air balloons were used to help capture a bird's-eye view of the terrain, but these were difficult and unreliable to control as well as being hazardous targets in the war years. The invention of the aeroplane opened up a whole new world for aerial photography of the landscape and assisted the military in land reconnaissance during times of conflict. As you look at your map, ask yourself if there is an obvious perspective from which your document has been created.

Did You Know?

The first topographical Ordnance Survey (OS) map showing landscape information was produced for Kent in 1801 and other counties soon followed using a scale of 1in to 1 mile. After a number of mistakes and resurveying, the OS map changed its scale to 6in to the mile in the 1840s.

Have You Considered?

If you've inherited an old map or have acquired one detailing areas of importance to your family, check for any 'age toning', the darkening of the paper over time. This could indicate that the map was originally either created on poor-quality material and was perhaps cheaper to buy when new or is the result of years of less than ideal storage conditions. 'Foxing' is a term for brown spots caused by damp or even impurities within the paper, while tiny holes may be the result of 'worming' when the larvae of insects have eaten through the paper while in storage.

Family hearsay may recount the stories of a map-maker ancestor. They may have worked as a colourist, a printer, an engraver or publisher, or could even have aided the work of a famous cartographer. Start your search using the census as a guide on sites such as *www.ancestry.co.uk*, and seek out the help of older relatives who may be able to shed light on the life and work of your forebear. Wills and old letters or correspondence may hold the key, or visit your local archive's library to check the historical directories, which may provide details of local publishers that could help your search. Alternatively, you can find a wide variety of directories online at both *www.ancestry.co.uk* and *www.historicaldirectories.org*.

What Next?

World maps help to give us some perspective on the countries around the globe, but to find information that is more relevant to our own family it is often essential to look a little closer to home. Printed ephemera in the form of 'tourist' pamphlets can be illuminating. They describe a location during a particular period and may include a map, often hand drawn and reproduced, showing places of interest and historical hotspots, perhaps with a description and details of which you had previously been unaware, even snippets of information about the local buildings and the residents at that time. It is worth scouring the internet, bookshops, fairs and car-boot sales for this type of memorabilia to enable you to set the scene in your mind of the locations where your ancestors and their families spent their lives. Who knows, they may even have been notable enough to be mentioned.

Old hotel brochures are usually only kept because the owner stayed there at some point and found their visit enjoyable. Perhaps there is a tariff included. Does the hotel still exist and are you able to follow in your ancestor's footsteps and arrange a visit? Weigh up all the questions that arise with the discovery of a map, brochure or similar pamphlet – just one random train of thought can lead you off in another direction of genealogical research.

Ask yourself:
* What made the location of your ancestor's map so important for them to keep it? Was it their home town or a favourite holiday destination?
* Are you able to date the map and does this tie in with the era in which your ancestor may have visited or resided in the area?
* Is it a specialised map of topographical wartime locations written in brief scribbles or outlined in detail?
* Could it have been secretly smuggled home from the front line in war?

* Is it an agricultural map giving a layout of fields owned? Is there a history of farming in your family?
* Perhaps your ancestors were landowners on a larger scale: does your example resemble estate plans of a location that was once in the possession of your forebears? Does it include the names of occupiers or tenants?
* Is your example a street plan marking a property or family business that now no longer exists?
* Could the map have been drawn during childhood, perhaps the result of a game or the desire to create a plan of their local area? A child's mind is usually inquisitive with an eye for detail so study the landmarks and places of interest they have chosen to include.
* Was your ancestor an avid walker with maps of different areas marked with their favourite routes or were they a member of a voluntary mountain rescue service where knowledge of the region was needed?
* Do you have an adventurer in your family tree whose explorations required a variety of maps to help them reach their destinations? Perhaps the passage they took is plotted on each copy.

From town plans to tithe maps, you can add extra dimension to your family history research. No matter what format your example takes, the information included can enhance your knowledge, from tracking down a specific street name to establishing the whereabouts of an inherited plot of land. Whether professionally printed, hand-drawn or part of a personal journal, unleash your enquiring mind and consider the purpose of the map in your possession.

SEVEN

CUSTOMERS AND COMMERCE: LETTERHEADS, BILLS AND RECEIPTS

Commerce changes the fate and genius of nations.

Thomas Gray

We all know that the census is perhaps the most valuable tool when trying to discover more about a forebear's occupation. We can look back at ten-yearly intervals to determine what employment they were in and whether the work was a family trade passed down through the generations from father to son or simply a means of earning money to keep a roof over the heads of their children. This documentation is, without doubt, essential, but what if the trinkets and memorabilia they left behind give more personal recollections of their occupational past.

It was not only in our ancestors' private lives that they left a trail to follow, but also in their working lives. Occupations and trades make fascinating subjects to research and related ephemera and personal souvenirs can give us a new perspective on an individual's career or their working environment. The tools that once belonged to a family carpenter or stonemason and now reside in your shed have their own fabulous story to tell. The wear marks and patina of the wooden handles will show that they were much loved and likely to have been the only means of earning money to provide food for the table and clothes for their backs. But other items can be just as valuable to the family historian.

The smallest article of ephemera can prompt a flurry of questions so it is worth writing a list that will enable you to tick off discoveries as you find them while working towards answering those questions that are a little trickier to solve.

Ask yourself:
* Did your forebear own his own business?
* Did they employ others? If so, how many and were they relatives or did they later marry into the family? (This is a more common situation than you might think.)
* Did they advertise their products or services offered?
* Did they take on apprentices and complete indentures for their training?

* Did they belong to a union or society connected to their trade?
* Did they contribute to trade journals?
* Did they own the premises occupied by their business and does it still exist?
* What were the tools of their trade?
* Do their account books, ledgers, headed letter paper or any correspondence still exist?
* Was their business/trade an integral part of the village or area in which they lived? Would they have been well known in the community? Could they have been recognised in local history books compiled on the area in which they worked?
* Do examples of their work still exist? (One of my forebears was a carpenter and a church lychgate he created still stands to this day.) Has the wall embellishment crafted by your stonemason ancestor, the weather vane made by your blacksmith ancestor or even the bridge designed by your engineering ancestor survived into the twenty-first century?

As you can see, it is not just a paper trail that you should attempt to follow; it is simply a case of 'thinking outside of the box' and looking for other lines of enquiry.

LET'S START AT THE VERY BEGINNING

Let's start, not quite with ABC as in the Julie Andrews song, but as close as possible, with the educational aspects of your ancestor's trade. An apprentice was a person who was bound to a master by an indenture for a specified period, from three to seven years, taking place between the ages of 14 and 21. This would enable them to become proficient in the skills needed to successfully accomplish their chosen trade. Both parties had to keep to this agreement, the master to teach and the apprentice to show a willingness to learn, or they could be summonsed by a magistrate's court to answer for their actions. An apprenticeship could be broken by mutual consent or by the death of the master, but where a partnership was dissolved the agreement could be taken over by others in the firm.

The term of the apprenticeship would be mutually agreed and the conditions laid out in an indenture. This was a legally binding contract written on one sheet of paper, in duplicate and separated into two halves. The edges of the document would be indented, hence the name, with each party retaining half, enabling it to be fitted back together to make a whole and thus confirm authenticity. The discovery of an indenture makes a wonderful addition to your family story, providing details of a period of your ancestor's life that is usually not recorded on any other document. Although these documents were common during Victorian times to make it possible for ordinary people to learn the skills necessary to become a tailor, blacksmith, weaver or a host of other occupations, the creation of apprenticeships dates back to the Middle Ages. Many of our forebears benefited from this system, but so did the masters, who enjoyed cheap labour in exchange for training.

TRADE JOURNALS

If your ancestor had a trade, try to establish whether any related trade journals were produced. These publications were created to help, advise and inform their readers employed in a particular occupation. They gave details of notable figures in that line of work, news of the latest developments or equipment, advertised positions, listed distributors and were generally essential for helping keep one's finger on the pulse before the advent of the internet.

From boilermakers and steelworkers to cabinetmakers, pawnbrokers and medical practitioners, there was a journal for almost every trade. They ranged in size from small A5 versions to tabloid proportions and were produced by industry associations or trades union. Most were printed in black and white, sometimes with a coloured cover and contained engraved images; some examples took on a newspaper format and called themselves periodicals or gazettes, such as the *Pawnbroker's Gazette*.

Nurses, bricklayers, brewers and coachbuilders all had their own professional magazine and although they were often produced in short print runs, they were highly sought after by those in an occupation who wished to keep abreast of the latest information. Lack of television and radio made them an indispensable means of communication that could be targeted at a more specific audience than by merely advertising in a general British newspaper. If the area in which your ancestor lived and worked was known for a specific trade, contact your archives or local history library

Occupational postcards can give us an insight into the clothes our ancestors wore during their employment in particular trades.

Trade journals are a fantastic find and can help us to understand more about our ancestors' occupation during a particular period in history. Look out for other occupational ephemera among your ancestors' belongings that may point towards a particular trade or occupation.

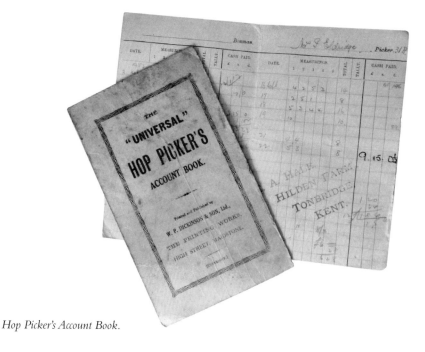

Hop Picker's Account Book.

to see if any back copies have survived and reside within their catalogue. If investigating online, use broad search terms, such as journal, gazette, periodical, along with the name of the trade if you are unsure of the actual title of a publication.

If a copy has been kept by your ancestor, scour the pages. These journals are a gold mine of information and can help you to understand more about the trade during a certain period of time, from inventions and working procedures to health–and–safety issues and union presence.

Ask yourself:
* What is special about this issue to have warranted it being kept? Was the individual mentioned inside, perhaps for an award or for speaking with authority on their subject?
* Are there any items circled or pages folded that draw your attention?
* Could this be where the individual found an advertisement and applied for a position of employment: the copy kept as a reminder of their successful application? Does it include details of the employer's name and address and does the business still exist?
* Did the individual work in a family business and does this issue carry an advertisement showing the type of services they offered?
* Was the copy kept for reference, with the reader interested in articles on new developments in their trade?

THE COST OF LIVING

With a little effort it is surprising what details you can establish about an individual and you might even be able to gauge their financial situation and their standard of living. You may wonder how a box of old receipts can be of use to you, but don't be too quick to set them aside. Simple research can help you to determine the cost of living at a particular time by comparing the receipts and the products and services bought. You can begin to confirm whether your ancestor was wealthy or of limited means and by using a variety of online calculators you can find out how long it would have taken them to earn enough in wages to pay for these items. Many people keep receipts from weddings or funeral services and these are a good indication of how much cash the individuals were prepared to spend. Grocery bills and household items can also help in your mission to build a bigger picture.

For an entertaining exercise visit *www.measuringworth.com/ukcompare/* where a calculator enables you to determine the value of the pound sterling from any year from 1830 to the present. Dig out your ancestor's receipts, ledgers, transport costs and wills in which specific amounts of money are mentioned and get an idea of what these sums would be worth today.

Ask yourself:
* ★ What could your ancestor afford to do?
* ★ Were they living beyond their means?
* ★ Were they wealthy and could they afford to invest their spare cash?

STOCKS AND SHARES

Perhaps you've unearthed a stock certificate in your family papers. The study and collection of this documentation is known as scripophily, with *scrip* meaning 'ownership' and *philos* meaning 'love'. Study the certificate to see what it can tell you. Some have examples of beautiful artwork and decorative engraving as a backdrop to the company name for which the stock was issued, and additional embellishments such as vignettes, cancellations and watermarks to prevent forgeries being produced. These certificates were issued to raise funds for the company. Some enterprises were eventually successful, and some merged with other businesses, while there were also those that faced the inevitable and went bankrupt. From mining and telegraphy to railroad construction and aviation, stock certificates have been issued for a multitude of ventures.

If you've inherited a certificate, take a closer look.

Ask yourself:
* ★ What product did the company produce and what was its historical significance at the time of issue? This in itself could provide clues to your ancestor's forethought and ingenuity in investing their hard-earned cash in a product that they believed had potential.
* ★ How many shares were purchased and what was their face value at the time? This could also indicate the financial position of your ancestor by the size of their investment.
* ★ Was the company successful and is it still in operation today?
* ★ Did any famous or even notorious individuals sign the certificate?
* ★ When was it issued?

You may not have uncovered a family example, but know that a particular ancestor dabbled on the stock market and wish to acquire a certificate to illustrate your ancestor's financial dealings. Stocks and share certificates are extremely collectable, not only for their company history, but for their decorative graphics. Scour online auctions and ephemera fairs for the perfect specimen.

Always consider the condition of the certificate. Enquire first about the degree of wear and tear, staining, creases and damage that can occur with any paper product and try to buy the best that you can afford.

Mortgage agreements, indentures and other conveyancing documents can all provide clues about properties owned, their locations and the parties involved in financial transactions. A little research may reveal whether the properties mentioned exist today and if they still belong to your family.

OCCUPATIONAL MEMORABILIA

There are numerous occasions when items were kept by a worker as a reminder of their time in employment. These examples were often indicative of the most popular occupations of a particular era. Some were given as rewards for excellence, long service or recognition of a task carried out, others were small mementoes that found their way into the pockets of the employee as a keepsake.

Pit Tallys

During the eighteenth and nineteenth centuries, the coal mines were one Britain's most prominent employers of men and boys. Long hours and dangerous conditions in an environment hazardous to health took its toll, shortening the workers' lives through the inhalation of coal dust and its related diseases. Today, we understand more about the health risks involved, but then it was a way of life. Your mining ancestors may have had little in the way of occupational tools to pass down through the generations, but an item that is easily overlooked and could well be rattling around at the bottom of an old shoebox or inside a jar of family trinkets is the 'pit check' or 'tally'.

Introduced to Britain between 1860 and 1870, the tally continued in use until the late 1980s when new gadgets such as the electronic swipe card came into force. Known by various names from tally and token to pass, pin, check or mottie, each familiarity depended upon the area of the country in which they were used. Manufactured from a variety of materials, including brass, aluminium or zinc (with some examples known to have been made in leather or Bakelite), each check was not much bigger than a pound coin and could vary in shape, whether circular or square, hexagonal or triangular. An identification number, the name of the colliery and sometimes the initials of the colliery owner were stamped onto each item and a small hole was drilled to enable it to be threaded onto a cord, chain or spike.

Buttons from an old uniform could give clues about a previous occupation and the company or trade in which your ancestor was employed. This example shows a small button from the London, Midland and Scottish Railway Company. (Stewart Coxon)

Initially, each miner would exchange a tally for a numbered lamp before he went down into the mine. On his return, he would replace the lamp and collect his tally. This system indicated which lamp was used by which man and was also an accurate means for the mine management to calculate how many men were down the mine at any given time, enabling a swifter rescue attempt in the event of a pit disaster. It also acted as an early form of attendance register as each tally was personal to an individual miner.

If you've discovered one of these fascinating items among your ancestor's belongings don't dismiss it as a worthless piece of metal. The tally is part of our industrial heritage and mining is an area of employment that has diminished greatly over the decades. Each tally recognises the work, hardships and perhaps even sacrifices made by every employee and the hand-stamped details give you another clue to follow.

Perhaps you hadn't even realised your ancestor was a miner. He may have worked in this trade for a short time between the census years and this period of his employment is not recorded. The tally will name the colliery at which it was used. Follow up this lead to see if you can find details of your forebear's involvement. A small number of tallies from different collieries may indicate that your miner moved around during his career.

What Next?

If you've already confirmed that your ancestor spent their life as a miner then collecting pit tallies is a great way to pay homage to their work. Tracking down those related to the collieries in which they were employed can be addictive. It is an affordable hobby, although like any collectables the prices increase for rarities. Due to their size, the space needed for storage and display is minimal. Get a feel for the examples offered for sale by doing your homework on websites such as *www.ebay.co.uk*.

Research further by visiting the UK's National Mining Memorabilia Association at *www.mining-memorabilia.co.uk/index.htm*. Everything from tallies and mining lamps to company letterheads and even mining equipment is discussed and you're guaranteed to find other like-minded collectors to help with your queries and offer advice.

Occupational memorabilia appears across all trades and forms of employment. Perhaps your ancestor was left a gift from her time as a domestic employee or nanny. Long-service awards, such as inscribed watches, fobs and tankards, may have been given in factory-based occupations. For those with a specific skill, it was commonplace for the individual to keep their own tools of the trade. Doctors would have their own medical bag and paraphernalia, carpenters would have had their own hand tools and tailors would prefer to use their own sewing equipment. No matter how small, clues to an ancestor's career may well have been left behind for you to find.

EIGHT

ARTISTIC ADVERTISING

Advertising is the greatest art form of the twentieth century.
Marshall McLuhan

Whenever we talk about inherited or collected paper items the word 'ephemera' is always mentioned and is a term used to describe handwritten or printed items that form part of everyday life. When first produced, these pieces were not necessarily intended for preservation but instead for the purpose of advertising or getting some form of information across to the reader. Examples include tickets, catalogues, programmes, packaging, newspapers, advertising leaflets, trade cards and much, much more. These little gems can reveal so much and reflect the mood of the day and the fashion of the times, or give us a glimpse into social history or an insight into a particular occupation. For the family historian who wants to bring a visual treat to their genealogical findings, albums or displays, they are essential. Once you start to look around you, you begin to realise what a huge area ephemera covers. As well as being evocative reminders of a forgotten era, ephemera can also point us in new directions of research.

PUBLICITY AND PROMOTION

Today, we rely on advertising to inform us of the best deals and products around, the destinations we can visit or the new gadgets we can buy. Whether complementary, advisory or in a warning capacity, advertising helps spread the word to millions of consumers by a variety of media from television and radio to magazines, newspapers and the internet. But before the introduction of television and radio and long before the worldwide web was at our fingertips, consumers relied solely on packaging, labelling and its visual impact on shop shelving or in periodicals of the day to learn about the latest products and services on the market.

Although eighteenth-century posters were informative to customers, with details of product names and prices clearly printed, they were far from decorative. It wasn't until the nineteenth century that printing methods improved enough to allow the addition of pictorial images and embellishments to draw the public's attention. These advances also meant that mass production could be achieved, enabling posters to become the accepted advertising medium.

Taking their lead from advertising postcards, first produced in 1869 and simply detailing the company's name and address, posters developed into illustrated, full-colour advertisements and began to command artwork of a very high standard. Top illustrators were employed to make the designs attractive and eye-catching, with the teamwork and discussion between artist and manufacturer ensuring that the products were given the best exposure in what was becoming an ever-growing, increasingly competitive market.

A great deal of thought was put into creating an image that would sell a particular product. Experts in the field declared that if the information on the poster could not be absorbed in two seconds then the poster was not doing its job. Humour was used in many cases to convey a message about the superiority of the product or how

An 1890s image advertising magnetic corsets. Perhaps you've discovered vintage advertising telling you more about the products and services used during a certain era. (The Advertising Archives)

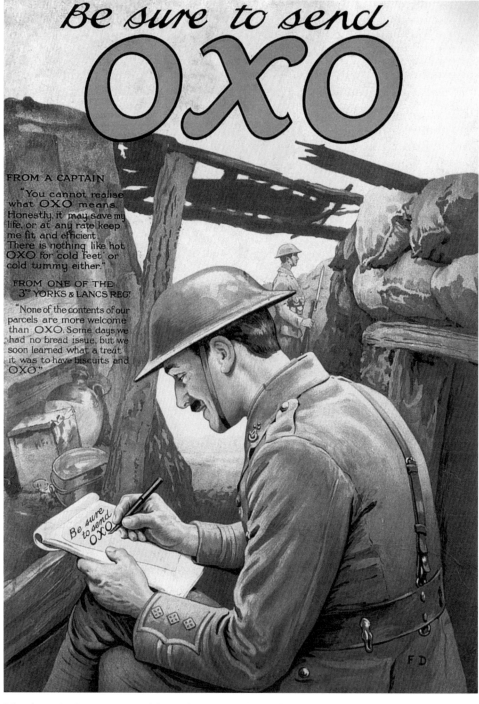

This classic OXO image was used during the First World War when the needs of the soldiers on the front line were promoted in the product's advertising campaign with the motto 'Be sure to send OXO'. (The Advertising Archives)

essential the service was, along with cartoon-style illustrations of men, women or children using the items advertised in varying situations. Bisto was famous for using this technique, while soap manufacturers preferred to use more endearing images to attract their customers. Other companies used catchy slogans or thoughtful phrases and illustrations.

Depending on the era, you may also get a feel for the period or the type of clientele the manufacturers wished to attract. The 1920s saw an array of feminist messages creeping in and the late 1930s and 1940s saw military and patriotic themes. All ensured that the product names were prominent and usually accompanied by a distinct and easily recognisable image, which, if the product still exists, is likely to be in use in today's advertising. Where the product was not quite so prominently displayed, clever marketing ensured that it was set against a complementary backdrop to further establish its quality, simplicity or other essential characteristic.

What Next?

If this kind of ephemera is where your interests lie then visit The Advertising Archives at *www.advertisingarchives.co.uk*. Established in 1990 by Larry and Suzanne Viner, it is one of the largest and most comprehensive resources of its kind in Europe. By viewing the pictorial images in their collections you will find examples from the mid-nineteenth century to the present day, enabling you to date items that you may already have and get a feel for particular areas of the subject that interest you. From British and American press advertisements and magazine covers to posters, advertising stills and postcards, this is a valuable resource to have at your fingertips and you may even be tempted to add some of their original ephemera to your own budding archive.

Perhaps most importantly, the Viners also offer a free valuation service, with Christie's and Sotheby's auction houses often referring their customers for expert advice. Why not take advantage of this facility? Although everything bequeathed by an ancestor is priceless to the family concerned, many items may have little monetary value, but don't fall into the trap of thinking that this applies to all of their possessions. You may have underestimated the worth of your paper memorabilia and specialist guidance could be just what you need. For further information contact: The Advertising Archives, 45 Lyndale Avenue, London NW2 2QB; tel: 020 7435 6540; fax: 020 7794 6584; email: *info@advertisingarchives.co.uk*.

PERFECT PACKAGING

Understandably, everyone intended for their products and services to stand out from the crowd. Manufacturers wanted their goods to make a statement on the shelves so packaging began to follow the same colourful and dynamic route as the advertising poster, enticing people to buy.

As a result, examples of these clever marketing techniques have become highly collectable today. Tins, boxes, bottles and jars carried distinct logos and designs and were kept long after the product inside had been used up. Such was the attention to detail that they were often reused by the purchaser, perhaps to store other items or just for their decorative appeal, and may well have stood the test of time and found their way into your ancestor's belongings.

Perhaps that old tin in which your grandfather's cigarette cards are stored was once a limited edition Huntley & Palmers biscuit tin, or your great-aunt's button

An example of advertising on ceramic packaging for Woods Areca Nut toothpaste from a chemist in Plymouth.

They may be a little battered and worse for wear, but it is surprising which types of packaging have stood the test of time. They give us an insight into the products our ancestors would have used. (Stewart Coxon)

collection has been passed down in a vintage Callard & Bowser chocolate box, with pins kept separately in a Player's tobacco tin that possibly held your great-uncle's favourite tobacco. This is a time to look beyond the contents and examine the actual packaging.

If you're intrigued to find out more about the packaging of a certain period then you could visit London's Museum of Brands, Packaging and Advertising (2 Colville Mews, Lonsdale Road, London, W11 2AR; tel: 020 7908 0880; website: *www.museumofbrands.com/visitus.html*). The collection provides a time-tunnel of consumer products and social history from the Victorian era to the present day. Arranged by decades, the displays enable us to see how Britain's styles, designs and technology have developed and how our attitudes and behaviours have changed. This is the ideal day out for the family historian who wants to see the types of products that our ancestors used in their daily lives first-hand. Thanks to the collection of consumer historian Robert Opie, you're guaranteed to see examples from travel and transport to food and fashion.

TRADE IT!

For sheer commercial creativity and artistic licence, the world of Victorian trade cards shows just how important public promotion of their products and services was to our ancestors. These decorative cards, given away by shopkeepers and merchants from the mid-1800s, advertised everything from sugar and sewing equipment to carpet sweepers and cough linctus. At that time, this kind of marketing was commonplace in America – evolving from the simple cards used by tradesmen in the late 1700s to advertise their services – but did not become as popular in Britain until around the 1880s when smaller cards were given away with brands of tea and cigarettes.

The Victorian passion for collecting led to many of these advertising artworks being pasted in scrapbook albums to create colourful and decorative layouts. As a result, the descriptions and images of just some of these products have been preserved and may well have been handed down within your family. Each small card gives us a glimpse into another world in which some foodstuffs were not as readily available or services not so prevalent as they are today. Are there clues as to your ancestor's favourites – perhaps a liking for confectionary, images featuring flowers or cards with a musical theme?

If you're inspired to add to an existing album then you have chosen to enter a highly collectable area of ephemera. From coffee and cocoa to soaps and shoe polish, trade cards cover a wide range of subjects. These historical gems can be found at specialist auctions and trade fairs held specifically for the buying and selling of these cards. Their artistic value alone can make them extremely sought after, along with the way that they reflect all that was new and innovative during the nineteenth century.

Track down items at antiques and ephemera fairs, where the opportunity to rummage in boxes underneath a stall may reveal hidden treasures within the pages of a tatty old scrapbook, or on auction sites such as *www.ebay.co.uk* (enquire thoroughly about the condition of the item before you agree to buy).

Decorative trade cards can help us to understand more about the products and services used by our forebears.

Purchasing Pointers

Do your research to get an idea of the current value of the cards you wish to acquire.

* Be aware that there are reproductions on the market so try to buy from a reputable dealer.
* Avoid any items with rips or creases and where possible always buy the best examples that your pocket will allow.
* Check the backs of cards to ensure that the advertising details have not been ripped away if removed from an album.

Once home:

* Care should be taken when attempting to soak off cards that have been glued to old scrapbook pages to avoid ruining nice examples – if in doubt seek advice from a dealer or experienced ephemera collector.
* Display in divided pockets or scrapbooks that are acid and lignum free to prolong the life and colour intensity of the cards.
* Store out of direct sunlight: avoid areas that are prone to damp or moisture.

NINE

PHOTOGRAPHY

Photography takes an instant out of time, altering life by holding it still.
Dorothea Lange, documentary photographer

Other than hand-painted portraits, photographs are the only means by which we are able to physically identify our ancestors' appearance. Descriptions such as 'hazel eyes, blond hair' or 'small scar to the right cheek' may appear on documentation such as identity cards or military records but for complete facial recognition, photographic evidence cannot be beaten.

Equally valuable are the photographic methods that can help us to establish the period in which a picture was taken and give us the opportunity to work out the approximate age of the sitter and crucially, establish an identity.

Step Back in Time

Initial Exposure

Today, we take photography for granted and are able to capture an image at a moment's notice on our modern cameras and mobile phones, but in the early Victorian era the process was still in the early stages of invention.

In 1837, Louis Daguerre discovered that by coating a copper plate with silver and treating it with iodine vapour to make it sensitive to light, he was able to generate a photographic image that was fixed, did not fade and needed less than 30 minutes of light exposure. He named the results of this technique the daguerreotype. Daguerre's innovation proved to be a breakthrough and overcame the previous problems faced by fellow inventors by lengthening the life of the captured image, preventing it from fading and ultimately disappearing forever. Four years later, in 1841, Britain's William Fox Talbot developed the procedure so that multiple copies could be made with the first negative-positive process, known as the calotype, where exposure was reduced to less than 2 minutes.

Over the years, the camera saw many changes to the exterior shell, shrinking in size from a cumbersome apparatus made from finely polished wood, brass and leather, to a more portable, hand-held device. Previously, owning a camera had been a luxury available only to the wealthy or professional studios, then in February 1900, the first mass-market gadget became available in the form of the Box Brownie, one of a series of inexpensive cameras introduced by Eastman Kodak. By pushing a button on its simple cardboard construction, the 'snapshot' was captured on the internal roll of negative paper, which could then be sent away for processing and printing. Eastman had already coined the sales slogan 'You push the button, we do the rest', but now the camera did not have to be sent away with the film so when a customer bought the Brownie they had bought a camera for life. Inspiring creativity, the compact device was extremely popular, capturing the imagination of millions of budding photographers eager to create memories of their own lives on film.

What Next?

First, you should try to identify the type of photograph you've got.

daguerreotype: These appeared in 1839, but had fallen out of favour by the late 1850s. They were produced on a silver-coated copper plate and have a mirror-like surface. Most examples are cased to protect them, usually in leather-covered wood until the late 1850s when a composite or thermoplastic case was introduced. A daguerreotype is perhaps the easiest of photo types to identify.

ambrotype: Developed in 1854, this type was popular for no more than a decade. Each image was produced on glass and was always cased. To aid identification, remember that the ambrotype will not have the reflection qualities of its predecessor, the daguerreotype.

tintype: Appeared in 1856. The image was produced on an iron sheet. Although early examples were cased, they were soon issued in paper sleeves to reduce the cost. From the 1870s 'chocolate plates' were introduced, which gave the images a brown hue.

carte-de-visite (CDV): These were extremely popular from their introduction in 1859, and remained in vogue until the early 1900s. The image was produced on thin paper, often with a sepia tone, and mounted onto cardstock. Cartes-de-visite, with dark mounts of black, bottle green, burgundy and brown embellished with gold edging, were popular from the 1880s. Previously, paler mounts had been preferred. The name of the photographer was printed in gilt on the mount below the actual image, with the studio address details often printed in an elaborate cartouche on the back. The cards can also be dated by their rounded corners, which replaced their square-cornered counterparts from the 1870s onwards.

cabinet card: Introduced in Britain in the 1860s, this card provided the opportunity for a much larger image, with 6½ x 4½in cards being the most common size. Like the CDV, the image was mounted on coloured cardstock with the darker colours being most popular between 1885 and 1895.

PHOTOGRAPHIC CLUES

The key to identifying individuals in a photograph is to establish the period in which the image was taken, enabling you to whittle down your list of likely contenders. Acquaint yourself with historical dress styles, read up on the fashions of the era you are researching and learn to recognise characteristic clothing trends that will help you in your quest.

Tight-fitting bodices, high necklines, straight sleeves, ruffed collars and skirt lengths all have their part to play in the fashion stakes of previous centuries. It is not just women that can be identified in this way: hats, waistcoats, trouser turn-ups, jacket lapels and even moustache styles can help place a male ancestor in a particular period. Below are just some of the iconic fashion styles you should look for.

1860s
Tight bodices, high necks and buttoned fronts. Lace was often used for adornment on the collars and cuffs, skirts were full. Hair was worn parted in the middle, tied low at the nape of the neck, sometimes with the addition of ringlets around the ears. Men wore coats and jackets that extended in length to the mid-thigh over a collarless waist-coat. Hair was often parted in the middle; moustaches were worn in a drooping style; beards were full.

1870s
Bodices were tight, following smoothly into a flat-fronted skirt. The back of the skirt was full with a bustle or train. Necklines were low and were complemented with hair-styles worn high with tresses and rolls, which were adorned with bows, ribbons and combs. For men, shirt collars were stiff, sometimes winged, and waistcoats and jackets were buttoned high on the chest. The fashion was to have some form of facial hair, either a beard or moustache or both.

1880s
Sleeves were narrow and necklines were severe, sometimes with a pie-crust frill that would remain in fashion until the turn of the century. By the end of the decade, the bustle had disappeared. Hats were small to fit on top of tight, neat hairstyles. Men wore slimmer jackets left open to reveal their waistcoats and the embellishment of their watch chains.

1890s
Bodices were tight with skirts gathered at the waist and falling naturally over the hips. Leg-of-mutton sleeves came into fashion and seemed to grow in size each year. The corsetry forced the women's hips back and bust forward in an 'S' shape. Tailored clothes became extremely popular for outdoor wear. Hair was swept up on the head with loose-style bangs and ringlets. By the end of the decade, the fussy adornments were gone and hair was worn in one large, loose bun on the top of the head.

1900s

Tailoring continued with a nod towards the masculine neck ties and shirt collars, which were given a female twist. Blouses were full-fronted with puffed and frilled chests. Skirts just brushed the floor and overall shapes were longer and sleeker, signalling the abandonment of the corset.

1910s

Broad-brimmed hats were popular with the ladies and were worn with skirts cut just above the ankle and smartly cut jackets reminiscent of the style of tailoring that would appear in the First World War era. Hair became shorter in readiness for the coming jazz age of the roaring twenties. During the war years many of the men involved would have their photographs taken in military attire to give as keepsakes to their loved ones while they were away.

Photographs, cabinet cards and cartes-de-visite are perhaps the only true likenesses you might have of your ancestors. Examine the style and type of photograph as well as the image itself to help you with dating.

1920s

Women wore comfortable clothes, enjoying shorter skirts and the opportunity to wear trousers. Corsetry was abandoned and replaced by looser undergarments: the emphasis was put on the boyish figure. Bobbed hair was the latest trend, adorned with elegant hairpieces or neat hats. Evening wear featured elaborate beaded dresses in a shift style. Men abandoned formal wear, hats became more rounded and sportswear was a popular relaxed look.

1930s

Thick, heavy collars adorned women's coats. High-crowned, brimless cloche hats were worn by most women. For the men, double-breasted suits became popular, with many choosing to complete their outfit with a trilby, homburg or boater-style hat.

Top Tip During the Victorian era and into the Edwardian age, girls usually wore their hair down until adulthood and skirts were not full length. Similarly, boys would wear breeches instead of full-length trousers. In group photographs the sitters would be arranged around the most prominent person in the family, whether that be the father, a mother and her children or a newly married couple.

PHOTOGRAPH STYLES

Portraits of the 1860s were often full-length poses. By the 1870s and 1880s, the camera had moved in closer to give a half-or three-quarter-length shot, with the subject perhaps sitting at a desk or with some sort of studio prop. By the 1890s, the style had changed again to the more popular head and shoulder shot, which focused on the sitter and showed the face in greater detail.

Photo vocabulary

vignette: A photograph in which an image is clearly focused upon but fades gradually to a soft focus or white at the edges.

Top Tip **Storage Solutions**
- Handle old photographs only by the edges to avoid moisture from your hands damaging the images.
- Remove elastic bands or paper clips that may be holding bundles of photographs together as they can weaken areas over time.
- Although created with light, photographs can also be destroyed by light so store or display out of direct sunlight. Where possible make copies of old examples if you wish to display them, in order to protect the originals.

Top Tip

- Avoid storage in humid conditions that may then become damp, as this will encourage mould growth and irreversibly damage your photos.
- Lay prints flat and fold in acid-and lignin-free paper to safeguard them while in storage. Search the internet for specialist suppliers of archival sleeves, which will protect both your prints and their negatives.

What Next?

If your ancestor was photographed in London and you want to find out more, visit the PhotoLondon archive website at *www.photolondon.org.uk/default.asp* which holds a fascinating list of studios, photographers and their biographical details.

For more information on dating your images, researching photographers and their studios, and to understand more about photography techniques in Britain and Ireland between 1840 and 1940, visit the website *www.cartedevisite.co.uk*. Packed with useful advice, this is the place to learn about the culture, etiquette and methods of photography over the decades, enabling you to perhaps identify and further value your own family albums and images.

Consider This

In the Frame

Before the invention of photography, the only real means of preserving an individual's appearance for posterity was to have their likeness captured on canvas. Although this was originally an avenue open only to monarchs or those of substantial means, portrait painting gradually became the choice of most notable figures, military leaders and prominent members of society, with the opportunity to commission slowly working its way a little further down the social scale.

Portrait artists would work in a variety of mediums from simple sketches in pencil, pen or ink to larger works in pastel, watercolour and oil on canvas. Depending on the wealth of the sitter, the artist may paint his subject in their own home or if he had his own studio, arrange for the sitter to come to him.

Have you inherited a portrait of your ancestor?

Ask yourself:
- ★ Who is the sitter?
- ★ Are you directly descended from them or are they from another branch of your family tree?
- ★ Are you able to compare photographs of other family members to establish a likeness?

* Is it known who commissioned the portrait? (Family members often commissioned this type of painting to celebrate a special event: a husband for a wife on their wedding anniversary, parents for a child's significant birthday, or to mark the start of a son's career. Does your picture hold any clues?)
* What was the sitter's occupation or social standing? Can you identify this from the clothes they are wearing or the 'props' that have been included in the picture?
* Was the portrait intended for personal use to decorate a home or was it intended to hang in a public building?
* To aid identification, can you place the painting in a narrow time frame to help you to support your theory of who the sitter is or to offer up suggestions for alternative candidates? As with photographic analysis, the sitter provides a visual guide for historians. Study the clothing and accessories worn, the fashions of various periods and the individual's general appearance and manner depicted.

Not everyone could afford or wished for a large portrait to be painted, but instead wanted a likeness of an individual that was both personal and portable. Framed miniatures fitted the bill perfectly and could be painted on paper, vellum, wood, porcelain,

Did your ancestors capture their lives on film? Has the photography equipment they used stood the test of time?

glass and even ivory. They were small enough to be carried on the person, concealed in a locket or brooch, or added to the cover of a jewellery or snuffbox. Miniatures were popular love tokens enabling the owner to remember a loved one when they were travelling far away or even deceased. They also helped to create a family gallery when hung on the wall as part of a group or placed in a display cabinet.

Despite the detail and beauty of these individual pieces, the introduction of daguerreotypes and the development of photographic methods saw a decline in artist-assigned work. But consider this: it is often more likely that a family will remember the sitter in a painting rather than the subject of an unattributed photograph. It took money to commission the portrait and time to create it and this is a story likely to have stayed with at least one branch of the family. The simple act of handing the picture down through the generations will have given it a solid provenance. Along with any oral evidence that your relatives may be able to recount, have any records survived that mention the original commission, such as a receipt for work carried out, a letter to request the commission or diary entries about the sitting?

Seek out professional help with dating to aid the identification of a mysterious relative by contacting an art gallery or museum specialising in portraiture. They may be able to point out specific details that you have overlooked.

Did You Know?

Although an art form since the mid-eighteenth century, silhouettes did not become popular until the early years of the nineteenth century. An image of a person, an object or even a scene would be cut or painted in an outline format with a solid, featureless interior. Bold colours, usually black, were used to depict a likeness and this may have been the way one of your ancestors chose to be artistically portrayed.

TEN

EVENTS, ENTERTAINMENT AND OPINIONS

Our most treasured family heirlooms are our sweet family memories.

Unknown

Not all of our ancestors were interested in keeping diaries of their daily lives or penning long letters to their friends and relatives. Despite this, you will often find that they did want to keep in touch, show affection or send wishes on specific occasions or events throughout the year, so decorative cards fitted the bill perfectly.

Step Back in Time

Passionate Prose: The Development of the Valentine's Card
Throughout the centuries, the celebration of love and romance has taken a number of forms, from the singing of tender verses by prospective lovers to the delivering of simple gifts by besotted suitors, but the giving of specially made cards written with feeling from the heart has proved to be by far the most popular.

This custom of sending paper greetings began in the early fifteenth century when written tokens replaced oral or musical messages of love. Initially known as a 'poetical or amorous address', they are believed to have been started by Charles, Duke of Orléans, in 1415. His involvement in the Battle of Agincourt had resulted in his imprisonment in the Tower of London and to pass the hours during his confinement, he wrote romantic verses to his wife in France. These poems are recognised as the first type of Valentine's message and more than sixty of his original letters still remain among the royal papers at the British Museum in London.

There are many other instances in history that tell of similar acts of love. Even Samuel Pepys, the famous chronicler of domestic life, made an entry in his diary on 14 February 1667 which described a surprise card he had been given by his wife that had a gold script love message written on pastel-blue paper.

Charles II of Sweden brought the 'language of flowers' to Europe from Persia in the seventeenth century and floral art combined with words of love became all the rage.

Vintage Valentine's and greetings cards can provide clues to relationships, as well as indicating birth dates and occasions special to the recipient.

With each flower foretelling romantic secrets, complete messages about affairs of the heart could be told from one bouquet. Dahlias told of dignity, yellow tulips of hopeless love, white lilies of hope and honeysuckle of devoted affection. But it was the rose that held the greatest symbolism.

The ancient Romans and Greeks had long identified the rose with the goddesses Venus and Aphrodite; Christians associated its five petals with the wounds of Christ, the 'red' blood of the Christian martyrs and even the Virgin Mary. Each colour was chosen to have a specific meaning, from gratitude and sympathy to beauty and mystery. The red rose symbolised deep love and respect and has become the flower associated with St Valentine's Day.

Cupid is another favourite image associated with the world of romance, taking the form of a mischievous child with a bow and arrow ready to ignite the hearts of prospective lovers. From the Latin verb *cupere* meaning 'to desire', this Roman god played a central role in ancient commemorations long before Valentine's celebrations took over. Cupid's Greek counterpart was Eros. As the son of Aphrodite, these iconic figures of romance gave us the words '*erotic*' and '*aphrodisia*'. Looking at these enduring images as well as the written words is key to understanding the secret meanings your ancestors may have wished to communicate.

By the early eighteenth century, Americans were making use of an English import known as a 'writer' and influencing the practice of sending love notes in their own way. The writer was a small booklet that contained pages of verses and terms of endearment which could be copied onto decorative paper and used with a personal message. Letters of love had developed into folded cards, which were becoming increasingly elaborate with each decade. At this time, most images had a religious theme, with the angel gradually progressing into Cupid and the sacred heart into the Valentine heart.

Early nineteenth-century Valentines were either hand-coloured, etched or lithographed images with sentimental verses. Many were commercially produced, but in some cases there was the option of buying component parts separately, which the sender would assemble at home to make a personalised card for the recipient.

With the outbreak of the Civil War in 1861, the need to send home heartfelt notes became more important and the illustrations reflected this difficult period, with images of soldiers parting from their sweethearts. Others included a small embellishment in the form of a tiny mirror so that once the card was opened the face of the recipient was cleverly incorporated in the design. These cards became obvious keepsakes and manufacturers acknowledged this by including 'pockets' for locks of hair, early photographs or other mementoes to be placed inside.

Numerous adornments and techniques used during production followed, from the addition of tiny imitation gemstones, ribbons and silk linings to gilt embossing, intricate cut-outs or pop-ups and three-dimensional moving parts. However, not all Valentine's cards were heartfelt and meaningful. The mid-nineteenth century saw an influx of cheaply made, less attractive examples, which spawned the comical but caustic range by New York printer John McLaughlin. Known as Vinegar Valentines, they ridiculed spinsters, mocked old maids and satirised the 'love token' industry in general. Britain had its own version known as Penny Dreadfuls, featuring unflattering rhymes and sketches. Thankfully, this less than flattering custom soon died out.

ARTISTIC INTERPRETATION

In Victorian Britain, receiving and displaying decorative cards became a recognised pastime and when the postal service introduced the Penny Post, it made sending these cards even easier. With the majority mass produced in lithographic format, it wasn't long before new trends were developed and photographic studios generated real images that could be hand-tinted at a later date. British artist and book illustrator Kate Greenaway became well known for her drawings in subtle shades of blue and green, producing a range of commercial Valentine's cards from 1871 for Marcus Ward and Co. Fellow artist Walter Crane helped to provide some rivalry and competition, while across the Atlantic, Esther Howland of Massachusetts followed British trends by creating some examples of her own.

Imports from successful and innovative manufacturers in Germany and America flooded the market with handmade honeycomb tissue designs adding dimension to the intricate pop-up versions, ultimately giving the consumer more choice. Look closely at your own examples. Can you identify the sender and recipient from the coded love note inside?

Did You Know?

These mini artworks required skill and dedication to create, and each decorative technique had a special name to describe the methods used.

acrostic: Include verses spelling out the sweetheart's name.

cut-out: Use sharp scissors to create a pierced effect.

fraktur: In the style of the illuminated scripts of the Middle Ages, these Valentines would be decorated with ornamental lettering.

pinprick: Made by creating tiny holes with a needle to produce a lace effect.

rebus: Puzzle-type verses where certain parts of the words have been removed and replaced by tiny pictures that resemble the missing text.

theoram: Images painted through a stencil: a technique perfected in the Orient.

Remember

Not all Victorian Valentine keepsakes were in the form of a card. Sailor's Valentines were produced that consisted of a selection of shells laid out in a decorative mosaic format and framed in a small glass-topped wooden box, usually made from mahogany. These were commercially produced in the West Indies and were popular with sailors who wished to bring home a love token for the women in their lives. The shell patterns often spelt out terms of endearment or featured a heart-shaped layout. The discovery of one of these mementoes could give clues to an early maritime career in your family tree that you had previously not known about.

Along with recognising Valentine's Day, birthdays, weddings, the christening of a child and other occasions were marked by the sending of a note of good wishes and later a card, or even a telegram. Special birthdays may have warranted a day out or trip to the theatre, with even the smallest items of ephemera from an enjoyable experience treasured for years to come.

In memoriam cards mark the passing of a loved one and are kept as a reminder of the individual.

Collected letters, correspondence and journals can all provide evidence of family connections, events, occupations, hobbies and pastimes.

THEATRICAL CONNECTIONS

Perhaps your ancestor's social life has not necessarily been an area you thought you could research, but with a little bit of digging you may unearth some information that could help you understand more about their character and what they found entertaining. Television gradually became accessible to the masses from the 1930s onwards; previously the cinema, theatre and even the music halls had been our ancestors' main forms of visual entertainment. Playbills, newspaper advertisement cuttings and programmes were often collected after attending an event and kept as mementoes.

Step Back in Time

The British theatre programme (sometimes known as the 'playbill') first became popular during the later part of the eighteenth century when a single-sheet leaflet containing a cast list and background information was given to every member of the public who purchased a ticket for the event, and was also handed out in the surrounding streets to attract interest in the shows. As these items were, in effect, free, they were printed as cheaply as possible to avoid too much extra expense. Gradually, the single page evolved into a larger booklet with the name of the theatre and the production on the front. Inside would be details about the actors involved, the dates and duration of the play, often with a résumé of the scenes and production credits. One or two advertisements may also have been included, but it wasn't until later that this form of sponsorship was exploited and extra advertising became standard by the end of the nineteenth century.

After the First World War and the social upheaval between the classes, the cinema had taken over as the most popular form of entertainment, leaving the theatre reliant on a middle-class audience. London theatre managers realised there was money around to be spent and began to charge for their programmes. The revenue made went towards the entertainment tax imposed on theatre tickets by the government in 1916.

By 1940, with the Second World War well underway, the government introduced restrictions over paper usage and the programme reverted to the single-sheet format, folded in half to allow variations in the layout. Programmes from this era are naturally highly sought after.

What Next?

For many Britons, attending a theatre production was a highlight of their week and perhaps at the time a little more affordable than today's equivalent. By scanning the programmes in your ancestor's stash you may be able to discover a pattern.

Ask yourself:
* Did they follow a particular actor or actress? The more famous the performer, the larger the crowd that would attend and, in some cases, ticket prices would be higher. The number of performances attended may indicate how dedicated a follower your forebear was.
* Did they enjoy comedies, romances or crime productions?
* Did they follow a particular playwright: Shakespeare, George Bernard Shaw?
* Were they more interested in musical performances or opera?
* Did they attend specific theatres close to their home area or travel further afield?
* From which period do the programmes date? Can you work out how old your ancestor may have been when attending these events? Would they have been married at the time and what was their occupation?
* Did they save their theatre tickets, perhaps giving dates as to when they attended? If you find two tickets to the same performance ask yourself who accompanied them. Could this have been a regular pastime or was it a celebration? Become a detective and try to find out more about your ancestor's social calendar.

MUSICAL THEATRE

If plays were not your ancestor's passion, then perhaps they enjoyed musical theatre. The ability to portray love, anger, sorrow and humour through music was highly addictive to the public, who were swept into the story with the power of the recital. The combination of drama, dialogue, dancing and music resulted in a thrilling evening's entertainment.

His Majesty King George V.

VISIT TO FRODSHAM

WEDNESDAY, JULY 8th, 1925.

Townships of Frodsham and Frodsham Lordship.

JAMES ILLIDGE, Esq., J.P., *Chairman.*   J. C. CRAGG, Esq., *Vice-Chairman.*

The Parish Councils of the above-named Townships having co-operated with Representatives duly appointed by the Councils or Parish Meetings of the following Townships: Alvanley, Kingsley, Kingswood, Manley, Norley, and Newton-by-Frodsham, are pleased to inform the Inhabitants as follows :

HIS MAJESTY THE KING

Will, on the 8th July, 1925, in travelling from Knowsley Park to the Royal Show, Chester, break his journey at 11-22 a.m. in the Main Street, Frodsham, opposite the Town Hall, and will be graciously pleased to alight from his Car whilst the Children, approximately 2000, from the Elementary and Private Schools of the above-mentioned Townships are singing the National Anthem.

His Majesty

Will be received by the Chairman of the Joint Councils, who will be presented to His Majesty by the Lord Lieutenant.

The School Children will assemble opposite the Town Hall in their respective places at 10-45 a.m.

Grand Stands will be erected with reserved seats thereon, two on the North side of Main Street, and one on South side, at the following prices : 4/-, 3/-, 2/-, 1/- Plan of same can be inspected and Tickets obtained from the Hon. Secretary, Mr. J. GEO. ASTON, Main Street, Frodsham, Tel. No. 60, between the hours of 10 a.m. to 12 noon, and 1 to 5 p.m., from 2nd to 6th July, excluding Sunday. No tickets will be sold after the 6th, or seats reserved, and the inhabitants of all the Townships are particularly requested to avail themselves of booking early, as the number of reserved seats is limited.

There will be free reserved seats for some of the Aged and Infirm People, who are requested to send in their names and addresses to the Hon. Secretary not later than Monday afternoon, 6th July.

The Ex-Service Men will march to their allotted space on the North side of Main Street, opposite the Town Hall, and the Boy Scouts and Cubs, and Girl Guides, Local Members of St. John Ambulance Brigade, and the District Nurses, will also be present, and allotted spaces provided for them.

The Inhabitants are requested to assemble early and to avoid, as far as they possibly can, encroaching on the various allotted spaces. They are also asked by the General Committee to Display Flags and Bunting, especially those residing in Main Street, who are also, at the request of Lord DERBY, asked to refrain from displaying streamers across the road.

They are also particularly requested not to cheer after His Majesty has alighted, in order that the singing of the National Anthem by the Children may in no way be interrupted.

The Tradespeople and all other Employers are asked to favourably consider declaring the 8th of July a General Holiday, so that their Employees may have an opportunity of being present.

His Majesty

Will return from Chester for Knowsley and will arrive at Frodsham at 5-58 p.m. going through Main Street in a Car with Glass sides as slowly as possible.

By the kind permission of the Directors of the Grand Cinema, Frodsham, Free Shows will be given during the Afternoon of the 8th July to all Children attending the Elementary Schools.

God Save The King.

J. G. ASTON, Hon. Secretary, Main Street, Frodsham.

O. C. KEMP, PRINTER, FRODSHAM.

Local posters and fliers were kept as mementoes of special occasions and events that your ancestor may have attended. These are likely to be rare and hugely important when documenting the area where your forebears lived or when trying to create a local history archive.

During the latter part of the Victorian era, William S. Gilbert (1836–1911) and Arthur Sullivan (1842–1900) were two of the greatest names in their field. Between 1871 and 1896, the pair collaborated on fourteen comic operas, including *The Pirates of Penzance*, *The Mikado* and *HMS Pinafore*. Gilbert wrote the words and Sullivan composed the music, providing a winning combination when joined by innovative producer Richard D'Oyly Carte. Although publicised as 'light operas', they were the start of what we now know as 'musicals'.

What Next?

For more information on the programmes of Gilbert and Sullivan visit the website described as 'The Home of British Theatre Memorabilia' at *www.c20th. com/gilbert&sullivan.htm* The site is packed with fascinating colour examples of programme covers, length of runs, details of matinees and cancellations, the theatres at which the operas were performed and the most notable suites of music. It is an indispensable resource if your ancestor turns out to have been a Gilbert and Sullivan aficionado.

POLITICS AND PRINCIPLES

How your ancestor chose to spend their spare time was unique to them and while some people enjoyed escaping from the daily routine and the hassles of the world with a little light-hearted entertainment, others chose to attend rallies and meetings in support of a cause in which they strongly believed.

SUFFRAGETTES

By looking at an ancestor's belongings it is possible to get an insight into their personality, their likes and dislikes, their beliefs and values. The smallest piece of ephemera can often hold the largest clue.

In previous centuries, women were forced to suppress their belief in equality in favour of the wishes of their menfolk and it wasn't until the fervent campaigning of the suffrage movement that they finally won the right to vote in the early part of the twentieth century.

The discovery of pamphlets, advertising or correspondence relating to the suffrage movement may provide the opportunity to find out about your female ancestors' political opinions and principles by researching this fascinating subject a little bit more.

Although feminist philosophers such as Mary Wollstonecraft (1759–97) fought for women's rights in the eighteenth century, it was more than 100 years later, in the first decades of the twentieth century, that the campaign for votes came into the public eye. The suffragettes exploited the media of the time to publicise their message, ensuring that images of fellow supporters and cartoon-style illustrations with captions appeared not only in the newspapers but also on postal items such as poster stamps (having no postal validity, they were placed on the envelope next to the official stamp) and post-cards, helping to spread the word worldwide.

Throughout their campaigning, the suffragettes tried to cause as much disruption as possible to attract the attention of the general public to their cause. Some supporters served short jail terms as a result of their actions and their sentencing had the effect of attracting even more publicity for the movement.

Ask yourself:
- ★ Have you discovered suffrage propaganda and ephemera among your family's treasures? The movement's official paper was entitled *Votes for Women* – did your ancestor own a copy?
- ★ Are there any stories that suggest your female ancestors were involved in the movement, attended a rally or even served a jail term?
- ★ Have you found any newspaper cuttings relating to a particular demonstration? Could they have taken part? Make enquiries and perhaps even visit your local archives to understand how popular the movement was in your area and if any of your ancestors were notable characters within it.

Political and religious beliefs, campaigns for social reform and demonstrations about unemployment can all be treated in a similar vein. If involved, your ancestor would have set aside their spare time to fight for and promote their particular cause. Look closely at any newspaper cuttings that have been kept, search for clues in letters to other family members and research into when related events took place.

Remember

The clues may not seem obvious at first, but they are there. The Victorians loved to create scrapbooks in which they pasted items of interest. Some of these were simply colourful displays, but others preserved significant items and memorable events from their lives. These scrapbooks are where you may find family greetings cards, theatre programmes, performance reviews, political opinions cut from the newspapers of the day and a host of evidence waiting to be unravelled or pieced together. By the Edwardian era, at the beginning of the twentieth century, the emphasis was changing and people began including their opinions, thoughts and beliefs, theming the scrapbooks to encompass their love of a particular subject or event of historical importance with the addition of their own notes and sketches. The discovery of such an item allows you to peek inside your ancestor's mind.

ELEVEN

A LASTING REMINDER

We do not remember days, we remember moments.
The richness of life lies in memories we have forgotten.

Cesare Pavese

If background story is what you are looking for then newspapers are definitely the place to start. The old suitcase under your bed or the shoebox in your grandma's attic may well hold snippets relating to your heritage, carefully removed from the original broadsheets. But don't feel cheated if there are none, this is perhaps the one area where you have the opportunity to track down your ancestor's 'fifteen minutes of fame' by seeking out the original documents, which are waiting to be discovered in our country's archive libraries and repositories. There is also the potential to own some of these primary sources of information by purchasing copies from specialist dealers. But for some of us, the legacy of a dusty box of newspapers may hold a stash of archival information relating to important periods of our family's history.

Throughout the nineteenth and early twentieth centuries, publications like *The Sphere*, *The Graphic* and the *Daily Sketch* reported global events and incidents, helping to give us an idea of the concerns and issues faced by our forebears. While detailed coverage described the people in prominent positions, accounts of working, living and social conditions were reported alongside explanations of the latest transport systems. Products were advertised offering miracle cures or newfangled labour-saving devices. These chronicles make intriguing reading in their own right, but once you consider that your ancestor lived through these periods in our history, each story takes on a new, more personal, meaning.

Step Back in Time

Without doubt, the most popular newspaper produced during this time was *The Illustrated London News* (*ILN*). The debut edition appeared on 14 May 1842, comprising sixteen pages filled with thirty-two woodcut illustrations. This first issue covered a fancy dress ball held by Queen Victoria at Buckingham Palace, the 'breaking news' of the Great Fire of Hamburg and a war in Afghanistan. Fashion, book reviews and horticulture were all included, but the main appeal was the images that accompanied each story.

Its founder, Herbert Ingram, used the publication as an arena for some of his own views, which, as a Liberal, included debates on the poor and factory laws and the plight of the mining system. At sixpence per issue, and covering topics that appealed to the man in the street, 26,000 copies of the first edition flew off the shelves with 1 million future copies having been sold by the end of the first year.

The main aim of the *ILN* was to report on major news items of the day. Births, marriages and deaths were all recorded, as well as in-depth accounts of various wars and coverage of events and openings.

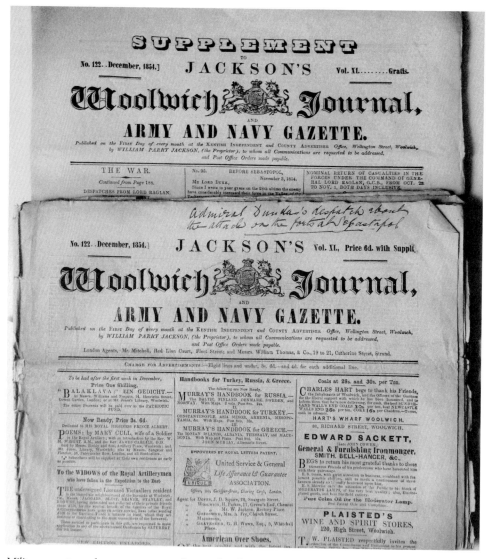

Military gazettes and newspapers reported news of conflicts as they happened. They can list casualties and fatalities as well as successes, honours and the progress of battles.

When the Duke of Wellington died in 1852, his funeral was transcribed in great detail. A year earlier, Joseph Paxton's designs for the magnificent Crystal Palace, home of the Great Exhibition, were reproduced, with Ingram's own reporters attending the event and contributing news for subsequent issues.

Littered with engravings, maps, charts and, later, photographs, this weekly periodical reported incidents not just in London, but around the globe. Ingram despatched six of his best war artists, including O.W. Brierly, to cover the outbreak of the Crimean War in September 1853. Accompanied by correspondents to report on the growing crisis, a war had never previously been conveyed in such detail.

What Next?

Special editions and supplements were produced throughout a newspaper's life and it is likely that if your ancestor kept a copy, then a special edition would warrant preservation. From this you can assume that they felt strongly about the subject reported. Perhaps they were a royalist and kept the edition marking the Diamond Jubilee of Queen Victoria in 1887 or her death in 1901.

Could they have followed the Crimean battles in Sebastopol and Balaclava in 1854 or the Zulu War in Rorke's Drift in 1879. Could family members have been involved in these conflicts? Did they monitor the exploits of Dr Livingstone and Henry Stanley in Africa, hinting at their own spirit of adventure, or were they more concerned with the fate of loved ones who had emigrated to America and could have been caught up in the San Francisco earthquake reported in May 1906? You will be amazed by the wealth of questions that arise once you start to look at the evidence left behind by our forebears.

The discovery of a single copy can provide you with world news and announcements, the latest fashions, details of food and household products used at the time and the mood of the nation. Where else could you reconstruct the past so vividly at just the turn of a page?

Did You Know?

The masthead of the *ILN* changed considerably throughout its life. Initially, the design was of multi-flagged barges, printed in black and white, escorting the mayor's state barge up the River Thames and past St Paul's Cathedral. Later, the number of barges was reduced and the masthead was printed in bold red ink with an elaborate border in the background. Not long after the embellished background was dispensed with, Big Ben made an appearance and by the end of the First World War, the typeface of the title was more streamlined, in keeping with the imminent 1920s style. By the 1960s, the pictorial banner was replaced with bold text. These changes are worth taking into account when looking out for examples from a particular period.

Colour editions of The Graphic *and* The Sphere *newspapers. (Stewart Coxon)*

DATES TO REMEMBER

During your research you may find it useful to know which other national newspapers were in production, but don't forget the many local editions that will provide details about your forebear's home town. The local archive library should be able to provide you with a regional list and dates of publication.

The Graphic	Weekly newspaper published under this title from December 1869 until 1932.
The Sphere	Weekly newspaper first published at the height of the Boer War in January 1900. Ceased publication in 1964.
Daily Sketch	Tabloid founded in Manchester in 1909.
Daily Mail	First published in 1896.
Daily Telegraph	First published as the *Daily Telegraph and Courier* in 1855.
The Times	Published in London from 1785, when it was initially known as *The Daily Universal Register*.
The Guardian	Founded in Manchester in 1821 by a group of Nonconformist businessmen and known as *The Manchester Guardian*.
The Observer	First published in 1791; the world's first Sunday newspaper.

FINANCIAL FACTORS

The age of a newspaper has very little to do with its value. What makes the difference is the story on the front page or any major events covered inside. Although local historians would be interested in events happening in their own particular areas, it is the larger incidents in British and world history that are likely to ensure that copies hold their value. Where thousands of copies were produced, the probability of editions surviving is greater, making them more affordable to purchase today.

Your dusty, slightly dog-eared example may be a rarity. Don't be tempted to dismiss loose pages. Your ancestor may have felt the need to 'cut out and keep' the beautiful engravings that were a feature of newspapers like *The Illustrated London News*, which used talented artists such as Louis Wain, Mabel Lucie Atwell, Kate Greenaway and Heath Robinson to create its images. Today, some of these can fetch well in excess of £50 per illustration, with some dealers specialising purely in loose pages from these publications. So do your research and make sure your issues are stored correctly to prolong their life.

STORAGE SOLUTIONS

The paper used in examples from the 1850s was a wood pulp. Early issues were unglazed, but later editions used glazed papers that allowed the printers to get sharper, clearer images. As a result, these newspapers don't deteriorate quickly so editions can be found in pristine condition. Remember that exposure to direct sunlight, moisture and extreme changes in temperature can cause them to turn brown, have areas of foxing (age-related spots) and even become brittle, greatly affecting their value.

Store in a cool, dry place in lidded boxes laid out in the fully open position so that the whole of the front page can be seen. When folded in half they can begin to separate along the crease as the paper becomes worn. For those with a higher value, special display folders can be bought.

If you wish to find out more about your copies, ask the advice of a reputable dealer and when purchasing further examples ensure you are buying an original and not a reprint. Be aware that it was sometimes customary to bind back issues using coloured morocco or calf leather, with gilding and cloth. These can be extremely attractive and enable you to get a feel for the news over a longer period.

Where to Find Out More
www.bl.uk/reshelp/findhelprestype/news/victoriannews/index.html
The British Library is a fabulous resource for finding out more about Victorian newspapers and journals.

www.iln.org.uk/iln_years/noframeiln.htm
A fascinating site about a collector's huge compilation of original copies of *The London Illustrated News*. Packed with articles, history and details about individual issues.

http://gale.cengage.co.uk/product-highlights/history/illustrated-london-news.aspx
A picture library archive dedicated to the newspaper with some intriguing insights into particular articles and full text searching of copies between 1842 and 2003. Although only available through institutions, your local library may have access.

www.ephemera-society.org.uk/index.html
Ideal for finding out more about all paper-related collectables.

Where to Buy
www.ebay.co.uk
A great place to see what is available and to compare prices. Many dealers list their shops on this site. Also search under 'antique prints'.

www.inprint.co.uk/thebookguide/fairs/index.php
Search for an antiquarian book fair near you.

www.abebooks.com
Searching here can put you in touch with dealers around the world.

www.etcfairs.com/ephemera
Gives details of specialist ephemera and antiquarian fairs held throughout the year.

LOCAL NEWS

For birth announcements, marriages, obituaries and regional stories, contact the archive nearest to where your ancestor lived and find out which newspapers would have been in circulation at that time and arrange a visit. Of course there will be the nationals of the period, but it is best to seek out the local issues that are likely to chart the goings-on of the area. In some cases, you will be able to view the originals. Ageing, dusty, browning and brittle at the edges, there is nothing quite like the smell of an old paper to whisk you back to a time when your forebears would have been turning the pages of a similar copy to read the news of the day.

In some libraries the newspapers are considered too delicate to withstand constant handling and they have been scanned and are available for viewing on microfilm. This can be a quicker method of searching the pages for that nugget of information, but can also prove quite tiring on the eyes. Whichever method you use, you are usually able to obtain copies of any reports you find.

Remember

If you visit with specific details that you believe should be included around a certain date, be aware that not all copies have survived. Indexes of a library's holdings will usually list their issues by year and often note which issues are missing. Also search those editions on either side of your chosen date; this is particularly important when the newspaper was produced weekly and the event may not have made the pages until one or two weeks later. Enlist the help of the archivist to find these indexes before you start your search.

WHAT AM I LOOKING FOR?

Newspapers *are* history. The freedom of the press ensured that there was very little restraint to their content so they are perfect for helping us to reconstruct the past, giving a reasonably faithful record of what events happened and how people at the time perceived them. We can also begin to understand how attitudes to death, religion, war, peace, culture and society as a whole have changed over the decades through the opinions quoted in the broadsheets and tabloids.

Pick any major event in world history and it is likely to have been reported in the journals of the time. Take a fresh look at your genealogical research and ask yourself how you can gain further information on your ancestors' lives by looking at the bigger picture via journalistic reporting.

Ask yourself:
* Do you know of any major event that took place in the area in which your ancestor lived? Was this reported and could your ancestor have attended?

* Are there any criminal connections within your family? Was anyone arrested, did anyone commit a serious crime, were they imprisoned, transported or even hanged? The proceedings are likely to have made local, if not national news. Witness statements are also an interesting resource when reported and can give details of a person's name and address and place them at a scene or location on a specific date.
* Did your ancestor take part in a wartime conflict? Were they involved in a particular campaign, allowing you to find out more precise details from the reporting, such as Gallipoli, Passchendaele or the naval Battle of Jutland? These events would have made headline news in the nationals, but incidents involving specific individuals would have also been picked up by the local newspapers in their home town. Always try to follow the smallest details and make full use of both local and national editions.

NEWSPAPER KNOW-HOW

As with all specialist subjects there is always a degree of terminology that can flummox the new starter. You may come across some of the following if purchasing your own original copies:

association issue: A newspaper that can be shown or proved to have belonged to someone of historical importance. Reliable provenance of ownership would be needed.

banner headline: The page-one headline, which is set in large bold type and stretches the full width of the page. This was commonplace from the nineteenth century onwards; before this, printing techniques usually meant that the headlines were rarely wider than the single column width.

copy: Not to be mistaken with the description of a reproduction, this instead refers to an 'example' or 'issue' of a newspaper or publication.

deckled edge: Before 1830, the rough, uneven cutting of the newspaper resulted in this natural edge to the handmade papers used for printing. Later, if the newspapers have been bound into multiple volumes, this edge can be lost in the trimming process.

disbound: A newspapers that has been removed from a bound edition. Look out for gluing at the spine or re-hinging at the spine with archival tape.

folio: A folio is made up of one or more full sheets of paper on which four pages of text are printed and then folded once to produce two leaves. In 1712, Britain imposed a tax on newspapers that assessed them on the number of sheets rather than the size of the sheets in each issue. As a result, the law became the incentive for creating large-format newspapers as a way of minimising the tax. During the eighteenth century, the largest folio measured about 12in x 18in, but by the mid-1800s this had increased to approximately 17in x 21in. Over the years many oversized issues have been produced, coining the descriptive terms 'horse blankets', 'elephant folios', 'atlas' and 'imperial'.

foxing: these are the brown spots that can occur when a chemical reaction has taken place between the impurities in the paper and the air. The cheaper the paper, the more

Examples of The Illustrated London News, *including a special commemorative copy issued in memory of Queen Mary. Could the discovery of such an example indicate that your ancestor was a royalist?*

probable the foxing. Light foxing is acceptable as long as it does not detract from the legibility of the text or the overall look of the item.

halftone: The method in which a photograph is reproduced in the newspaper as a printable image.

masthead: The decorated area at the top of the front page of the newspaper where the title and other vital information are printed. The text of some mastheads can be more ornate than others and can include a publication's founding date, slogan, logo and contact information.

octavo: The smallest size of newspaper and the regular size for most book formats and pamphlets. Approximately 8in x 10in in size, the term is often abbreviated to '8vo'. Measuring 12in x 17in, the large quarto is the size of most popular nineteenth-century illustrated weeklies and also of today's tabloid newspapers.

plates: The illustrations in each copy, which were created by engraving and cutting images onto copper and later, steel plates, and were then inked and printed onto paper. Eighteenth-century illustrations were often created by illustrious plate engravers such as William Hogarth and Paul Revere.

Whether examining handed-down copies, viewing examples at an archive or adding to your own family collection with originals, newspaper and periodicals cannot fail to educate, illuminate and inspire your genealogical quest.

TWELVE

CHANGING FASHIONS

Fashions fade, style is eternal.

Yves Saint Laurent

Understanding how our ancestors dressed throughout different periods in history is key to helping date any photographs we may have. It can help us to ascertain the approximate age of a known relative or can enable us to whittle down the possible identity of an unknown individual. The knowledge we have gained from the Photographic Clues section in Chapter 9 is intended to make us aware of the fashions of different eras and which design styles may have been popular. Let us briefly review our timeline.

From the subdued colours and restraints of Victorian style to the flamboyant glamour of the 1920s flapper dress, it is now time for us to become dedicated followers of fashion. This is the point where you need to use your skills to look beyond the faces in your photographs to the garments and accessories worn and any clues visible in the background.

The shape of sleeves, the length of skirt, the style of suit and the width of the hat brim are not just attractive to look at, they provide a time frame during which the photograph could have been taken. Most pre-1930s photographs were produced in sepia or black and white so we don't have the benefit of colour to go by, but this helps to concentrate our minds on shapes, style and accessories.

The Edwardian era of the early twentieth century saw the disappearance of the bustle and the return to the hourglass figure. Women became shapely once more, with the emphasis on a natural bustline and curved hips, aided by the corset. Necklines were high, often with neat collars, and waists were extenuated with a belt or sash. Tailoring was extremely important at this time – not only for men but for women too – with masculine clothes such as the shirt given a female twist with a high collar and fitted waist, which was extremely flattering on a woman when accompanied by an abundance of wavy hair swept up on the head and topped with a wide-brimmed, highly decorative hat. The overall look was more feminine than its Victorian predecessor: soft yet smart.

For the men, the long lean look of their outfits continued, with waistcoats fastened high up the chest and shirts with stiff collars that were often winged on formal occasions.

This era saw the introduction of the trouser turn-up, while lounge coats replaced the more formal frock coat. The fashion for beards was still in evidence, but they were now worn slightly less pointed, while moustaches were sometimes curled upwards. The bowler or homburg hat completed the outfit and top hats continued to be worn on formal occasions.

When the twentieth century dawned, fashions began to transform quite rapidly. Changing times meant that women threw off the shackles of the Victorian era and with tentative steps through the Edwardian period, long-length, figure-hugging clothes began to disappear. The restrictions of the corset and skirts made from reams of fabric were replaced by the shift dresses of the 1920s, while the hemline began to rise and embellishments changed from modest to magnificent. The period following the First World War was a time for celebration and it was reflected in the clothes and accessories worn. Patterns, colours, mixed fabrics and beadwork were a welcome arrival and a fresh approach to female style.

PHYSICAL EVIDENCE

Looking beyond the photograph, perhaps a prized garment has been passed down to you that was of great sentimental importance in your forebear's life. This could have been a wedding outfit, an occupational uniform or even an item of military attire, the latter being a significant aid in helping to determine in which conflict the wearer was involved.

With the majority of inherited clothing there is almost certainly a story to tell: it is just a case of looking at the item from a different perspective. The fact that it has been packed away and stored for decades implies that it was too expensive to dispose of, that an embellishment or the material was deemed to be beautiful and in need of preservation or, more importantly, that it had sentimental value to the wearer, who may have worn it for an occasion or family event and perhaps wished their descendants to do the same. By examining the fabric and the design of your example you may even be able to establish whether your ancestor was wealthy or of limited means.

From the Victorian era onwards, examples of collectable clothing are plentiful and if you have a garment or accessory from an earlier date, you are very fortunate indeed.

What garments are likely to have been preserved and why?

For the average Victorian, families tended to be large. Lack of nutrition and poor sanitary and housing conditions resulted in the spread of disease, with illnesses like cholera and tuberculosis being commonplace. Infant deaths and high mortality rates meant that attending the funeral of a loved one was often a regular occurrence. Women were expected to wear mourning clothes, so those dresses that have stood the test of time are usually in the sombre colours of black, brown or grey – giving the impression that the fashion world of the 'ordinary folk' was a very dreary place indeed.

Made for Mourning

For the female population, Victorian mourning etiquette was extremely strict. Clothes were dark and drab to reflect their sorrow and loss and the black outfit known as a 'widow's weeds' required a plain crêpe dress, bonnet and cloak to be worn without lace or trimmings. Crêpe was light in weight, but had an unusual crinkled surface that did not sit particularly well if the wearer was caught in the rain. Gloves, veils, caps and bonnets were also black in colour, representing the absence of light in the widow's life, although white fabric could be added at the collars and the cuffs.

After a respectable period, the woman passed into half mourning: the length of mourning depended upon your relationship to the deceased. Grey, purple, mauve and varying shades of lilac could be added to the wardrobe, with deep reds and burgundy being a popular choice towards the end of the era.

Rules were not so limiting for the men, who could get away with wearing the dark suit that they usually wore with the addition of a black hat, cravat and gloves, while children wore either black or white outfits with the addition of discreet black ribbons.

Bridal Attire

For those who married, the wedding dress would have probably been their most treasured possession. Although white has traditionally been the colour of choice, this has not always been the case and many of our ancestors have wed in a variety of shades, from blue right through the colour spectrum to brown. It was Queen Victoria who started the trend for white by marrying in a sumptuous white Spitalfields silk gown trimmed in Honiton lace and embellished with orange blossoms, setting the standard that, in the majority of cases, has remained to this day. Before Victoria enforced approval with her fashion statement there was a popular old English poem that told of the bride's fate depending on what colour dress she chose to wear.

> *Married in white, you will have chosen all right.*
> *Married in grey, you will go far away.*
> *Married in black, you will wish yourself back.*
> *Married in red, you'll wish yourself dead.*
> *Married in blue, you will always be true.*
> *Married in pearl, you'll live in a whirl.*
> *Married in green, ashamed to be seen,*
> *Married in yellow, ashamed of the fellow.*
> *Married in brown, you'll live out of town.*
> *Married in pink, your spirits will sink.*

For the majority of our less-affluent ancestors, it would not be until the 1890s and the increase in shopping outlets and drapers that women could even consider purchasing a white dress, but even then, most would opt for a colour that was more practical and could be worn on other occasions after the big day.

By the Edwardian era, the styles became even more ornate, but these extravagances were short-lived due to the outbreak of the First World War. As women's roles in society changed, styles became simpler and restrictive laced corsets became a thing of the past. Money was tight and manufacturing was focused on products that would help the war effort, so some brides chose to marry in their 'best' dresses in hurried ceremonies before their loved ones went off to the front line. The simple outfit that you have discovered in your loft may well be the much-loved wedding attire of forebears who married on the brink of the First World War or while their fiancé was briefly home on leave. This may have also been the case during the Second World War, when most brides thought it to be their duty to give up the traditional wedding and wear an alternative outfit or hire a dress solely for the ceremony. If both bride and groom were involved in the military at this time, they would often have been married in their respective uniforms.

After the war a new era began and with the ceasing of rationing and a gradual restoration of prosperity, the luxury wedding regalia established by our Victorian forebears returned.

Fashionable photography. By studying the fashions in your photographs you can begin to date and possibly identify the sitters. These cabinet card examples are perfect for scrutinising.
Left: Look at the style of hat and neat hair, the neckline and shoulders of the jacket, the pince-nez glasses.
Middle: The cut of the man's jacket, turned-up collar, waistcoat, watch and chain, and the style of his beard and moustache all provide clues as to the period.
Right: The woman's full-length pose, showing off the bustle of her dress, high neckline, bodice and hairstyle, helps to provide a timeline for dating the photograph.

Dating a Victorian Wedding Dress

Study the garment for the quality and type of material: does it comprise lace, tulle, organza, silk? Is there the addition of beadwork, pearls or other embellishments? Dresses from this era usually had fitted bodices, narrow waists and full skirts aided by a hooped petticoat worn underneath. Victorian women were known for their layering of clothes. Is your dress accompanied by undergarments such as a corset, chemise or additional petticoat?

Styles varied considerably throughout Victoria's reign, but from the late 1800s, when the white dress was seen as high fashion, the neckline may have been modest and the corset would give the effect of pushing the bosom upwards yet pulling the waist in tightly. Examine the size of the dress to establish how tall, and probably petite, your ancestor was, using the hemline, which would have been floor-length, as a guide. Bustles were introduced to the garments during the latter part of this era.

If your Victorian ancestor wed in white it helps us to establish that they were financially comfortable, as white was not a viable option for the poorer classes.

INFANT APPAREL

How things have changed over the last 200 years in the way we dress our babies. At the beginning of this period there was no such thing as a disposable nappy or Babygro. During the Victorian era most mothers made their newborn's garments by hand, often using white cotton material with intricate tucks and gathers to create a delicate pattern. It is hard to imagine the number of hours it would have taken to produce some of the more detailed outfits with their numerous pleats, hand-smocking and ruched bodices: techniques that were used on petticoats and nightdresses as well as for elaborate christening gowns.

At this time, babies wore long gowns until the age of six or eight months, when they were shortened to allow the baby to crawl. White cotton was practical as not only did the neutral colour suit the daintiness of the child, but it could stand constant boil washing at high temperatures and the pounding with the wooden dolly to help remove dirt.

Christening gowns are often passed down within a family so that each generation can benefit from wearing these handmade labours of love on such an important religious occasion. If this is the case in your own family, closer inspection can confirm whether the tiny stitching was done by hand or by machine. Perhaps one of your relatives may even know who made the gown originally.

PERFECT PRESERVATION

The care taken to store any garment of this type will make a huge impact on its future condition. Mildew can appear on cotton that has been kept in a damp atmosphere, while moth damage results in small holes that can be very difficult to repair invisibly. If you discover a stain or a faint musty odour or wish to remove a generally grubby appearance and feel confident enough to launder the item yourself, then wash by hand with a small amount of soap flakes or non-biological washing powder in warm water. Take care to rinse it well and let it dry naturally – not with the aid of a tumble dryer. Iron gently on a cool setting, placing a damp cloth between the iron and garment for added protection or on the back of the item if there is a lot of embroidery and pleats that you don't want to flatten. Starching can help to improve the appearance of the item and can also act as dust repellent. Wrap in acid-free tissue, box up and store well away from extremes in temperature.

When dating baby garments consider that from the beginning of the Victoria era the overall length of the gown was sometimes as long as 40in, while sleeves were short and necks were scooped and low. As the decades passed, the overall length decreased, necklines became higher and the sleeves gradually became longer. Thin, irregular, pearl-shaped buttons or matching fabric-covered buttons were used to provide a fastening, or alternatively a large sash was used to tie the garment together at the back. Remember, both male and female babies wore gowns or dress equivalents up to the age of 4 well into the early part of the twentieth century.

As the years progressed, baby gowns became plainer, but there were always the more elaborate examples made from lace, satin, silk, broderie anglaise, voile and embroidered net. On their christening day, Victorian babies were subjected to multi-layers of clothes from 'binders' – strips of flannel wound around the body to support and encourage straight growth – to a vest. There were also one or two petticoats and finally the christening gown itself.

By the 1940s, rationing dictated that decoration was kept to a minimum and the length of the gowns became much shorter. Fabrics changed from white cotton and fine lawn to a much coarser version established earlier in the 1920s, paving the way for the introduction of man-made fibres from this period onwards.

What Next?

If you have christening photographs of various members of your family, compare the images to see if a specific gown was customarily worn. Ask relatives if the garment still exists or if they know who the custodian is today.

MILITARY DRESS

Pride played a large part in the type of clothes our ancestors decided to keep and military uniforms fall into this category. Learning more about this specialist clothing can help you to date an outfit, link it to an individual and understand a little about a conflict in which they may have taken part and which, perhaps, shaped their lives and those of future generations. Some people carefully packed up the military attire of a loved one who may have died of injuries received in battle, while those who were fortunate enough to survive may have kept the uniform as a reminder of a significant period of their lives.

Colour Co-ordination

Originally, red uniforms (redcoats) distinguished British soldiers from those of other nations. Red dye was cheap and chosen as a bright colour to help lift the soldier's morale. Some believed that the colour was used to hide bloodstains, but this was not true as any blood loss usually showed as black on red fabrics.

With the adoption of rifles in the mid-1800s, visibility was now a consideration. On 30 December 1885, soldiers wore red tunics for the last time, instead trialling the khaki colour we know today, which provided better camouflage. The new colour was officially adopted in 1902 and from then on red uniforms were only worn as ceremonial dress.

The first uniform for naval officers was introduced by Lord Anson in 1748 and comprised an embroidered blue coat, which was supposed to be worn unbuttoned, teamed with white breeches and stockings. From 1825, these stockings were replaced with trousers and by the mid-1800s, the ratings, or ordinary sailors, were supplied with regulation bell-bottomed trousers that became wider from the knee down.

With developments in aviation and the formation of the air battalions in the early 1900s, it soon became apparent that those employed in the Royal Air Force required specialist clothing, with airmen adopting goggles and helmets for protection and leather jackets and fleece-lined boots for warmth in the open cockpits. It was not until the 1930s that enclosed cockpits provided greater shelter and allowed flying suits with detachable liners to be worn. During the Second World War, a wild bilberry known as a whortleberry was mixed with damson skins to dye RAF uniforms.

Jocular Jargon

It wasn't long before the service personnel began to have their own nicknames and descriptions for the garments and equipment worn. 'Scrambled egg' was the term for gold oak-leaf embroidery on the cap peaks of senior officers. 'Hairy Mary' aptly described the rough and prickly texture of the serge clothing that was often uncomfortable to wear, and 'fruit salad' was the name for the brightly coloured strips of medal ribbons worn on the left breast of the jacket. 'Tapes' were the woven lace chevrons worn on the sleeves to denote ranks of non-commissioned officers. 'Rings' were the different widths of woven lace worn by officers either around their cuffs or as shoulder straps on jackets to denote rank.

You may not have come across a full regimental outfit, but there are many accessories that have survived wartime conflicts and lived to tell another tale. Look out for belts, arm bands, hats, cloth titles, insignia and gloves. These smaller items could easily have been brought home and stored away without taking up too much space.

SENSIBLE STORAGE

There are a number of factors that can affect your garments in storage so before you prepare to pack them away, always make sure they are as clean as possible and follow the tips below to preserve them for the next generation.

* Remove dust by covering the item with a thin mesh or muslin and hoover very gently through this on a slow speed.
* Dispose of small insects that may have found refuge in the garment.
* Air well in a ventilated room to remove musty odours. Do not hang the garment outside in direct sunlight. Light can affect textiles causing the fading of colours, yellowing in white and cream garments and fragility in the fabric fibres, so try not to expose your treasure to a further spell in the spotlight that could ultimately shorten its lifespan.
* Depending on the type of material and its condition, consider whether you want to wash it. Is the fabric fragile? Is it covered in trims, ribbon or beading where the stitching may disintegrate on contact with water? Don't rush into thinking that you must wash and iron the item: some vintage pieces are better left in their natural state. Cotton, linen and some wools can be washed and, in some cases, dry cleaned before storage, but don't put them in the washing machine. Only ever hand wash, always be gentle, don't use harsh detergents and don't agitate the item to remove the dirt – you could do more harm than good. Rinse the item thoroughly.
* Avoid washing silk or attempting to remove stains without getting expert advice first and do not expose it to excess heat. Consider hanging creased items over a bath of steaming water – this can be particularly successful in garments made from velvet.
* Finally, wrap the item in plenty of acid-free tissue paper. Gently, but not forcibly, pad out shaped objects like cloth shoes, slippers and puffed sleeves to help them to retain their shape and roll delicate lengths of fabric and lace to prevent creases. Consider covering larger items in pure cotton or linen sheets. Ensure beaded or lacy clothing and embellishments that stand proud of the garment are also well covered with tissue to avoid imprints on other areas of the clothing. Do not use plastic as your vintage garments need to breathe to prevent moisture forming inside when packed.
* Where possible use purpose-made cardboard boxes to store the piece. Always buy a box big enough to avoid excess folding of the material.
* To enable air circulation, store unsealed in a place of consistent temperature. Try to avoid lofts and basements where possible, and every twelve months take time to check the garment over to ensure that moths haven't taken a fancy to your prized possession.

THIRTEEN

DECORATIVE ESSENTIALS: ACCESSORIES, JEWELLERY AND WATCHES

It is the unseen, unforgettable, ultimate accessory of fashion that heralds your arrival and prolongs your departure.

Coco Chanel

We may not have been fortunate enough to have uncovered a distinct piece of clothing from an ancestor's wardrobe, but instead are far more likely to have ended up with a small adornment worn to accessorise an outfit either on a special occasion or as part of everyday life. From hat pins and parasols to handbags and hair combs, these decorative items give us clues to an individual's taste, style and general appearance.

No matter what the century, most women tried to look their best with the resources they had. Embellishments and adornments were used as a way of enhancing the appearance and complementing their ensemble. The fashion for long hair that could be tied up and arranged in a multitude of styles meant that decorative clips and combs were much in demand. Ranging from small examples that could fit in the palm of your hand to larger pieces that made a statement, the item you may have discovered could easily transport you back to another era. Even in the roaring twenties, when short, bobbed haircuts were the trend of the day, art deco-style accessories made from silver, enamel or Bakelite were extremely popular.

HOW WOULD YOUR ANCESTOR HAVE WORN THEIR HAIR?

The nineteenth century
Following the eighteenth century – which had been dominated by decadent powdered wigs, ringlets and high coiffures, with all manner of extreme embellishments from mini sailing ships to imitation nesting birds – the nineteenth-century Victorians took a much more controlled approach. Hair was worn naturally and was combed to create sleek,

smooth lines, wound and plaited into elegant yet demure styles. Fringes were usually worn short and curls were kept under control. Black bows and ivory combs were all the rage at the beginning of this era, a trend that continued when the queen was in perpetual mourning dress after the death of her husband, Prince Albert. Respectable women were rarely seen with their hair worn loose, which would have been considered vulgar, but instead went for neatness and restraint and discreet embellishments.

Early 1900s

Preferring a softer, more feminine look, Edwardian women of the early 1900s wore their hair in full, somewhat 'puffy', styles, loosely piled on top of their heads. To balance this fashion, large hats were worn, sometimes trimmed with ostrich feathers and kept in place with decorative jewelled hat pins.

The 1920s

The introduction of the flapper style in the 1920s saw the most drastic change in women's hair styling and the bob emerged as the ultimate fashion statement. Cut short, the style could either be worn with a gentle wave or slicked back for a more formal look. Headbands decorated with jewels, beads, sequins and feathers completed the elegant appearance.

The 1930s

The 1930s saw the re-emergence of the shapely female body after the boyish form of the previous decade. To complement this, women wore their hair in soft, sultry waves adorned with hats that helped expose their faces. The need for more waves increased as the decade developed and the hair was firmly fixed in place by curling small sections around the finger and securing them with a hair pin – these were known as 'finger waves'.

The 1940s

Soft curls and romance were the fashion in the 1940s, with natural wavy looks that mimicked women's silver screen idols. Plastic hair rollers and styling lotion were used to help create the curls and there was very little call for hair accessories. During the war years, many women worked as land girls or took on the manual jobs and munitions work left by their menfolk who had gone off to fight. To keep their hair tidy they wore headscrarfs knotted neatly at the front of their heads above the fringe, scooping up their hair from the base of the neck.

What Next?

Study photographs of your ancestors. Their hairstyles may well help you to date them.

PARASOL PROTECTION

It wasn't just the outfit and accessories that were important to a woman's appearance, but also their facial condition. Up until the 1920s, ladies would not be seen out in the sun without a parasol to protect them from its rays because, unlike today, trends dictated that it was extremely unfashionable to have tanned skin or freckles.

Maintaining parasols was essential and women would often have them re-covered, not just when they were worn out and the fabric looked a little tired, but also to change the colour scheme and fabric to match a particular outfit. Tassels, lace, net, ornate borders and simple decorative bands were just some of the adornments that could be added. From satin and silk to cheaper cotton twill, the parasols varied in shape and elegance from small-sized examples with long tapering handles to oriental pagoda-style domes or paper-covered designs splashed with exotic motifs. For most women, the parasol was all about show and making a statement so even the lining was created in a different colour from the exposed material for maximum impact.

It can be hard to date a parasol precisely unless the collar around the handle was made from gold or silver and hallmarked, but such a possession can give the impression that the owner had a sense of style and appreciated beautiful items. A close examination of the quality of the craftsmanship and the materials used can reveal whether the parasol was well made and expensive to purchase. Delicately carved handles and precise attention to detail are paramount, but don't forget to look inside.

Are there patches around the stretchers to help protect them from wear? Are the ribs that support the covering well made and in a good state of repair? Be aware that renovation of these can be costly. Is there an ornately carved knob on the handle, or is it topped with a precious stone, painted-porcelain or cut-glass decoration? Does your example conceal a powder puff or perfume bottle in the handle? The quality of the item offers clues as to the financial situation of the owner or her family. Most working-class women would not have used a parasol.

These collapsible canopies were made not only to shield women from the sun, but also to repel the rain, and were just as fashionable for men to carry as for their female counterparts. Although the working mechanisms are generally the same, the major difference is the material used to cover them.

Step Back in Time

The word umbrella derives from the Latin *umbella*, with *umbel* describing a flat-topped flower and *umbra* meaning shaded or shadow. Similarly, parasol can be broken down into *para* meaning stop or shield and *sol* meaning sun.

Despite being an essential twenty-first-century item, umbrellas are an ancient invention and images of the device were represented on early Greek vases and depicted on some of the great monuments of Arabia. Egyptian pharaohs were often portrayed in the shade of an umbrella to symbolise their royal power and priests used basic contraptions as part of both religious and ceremonial regalia. Even the

Aztecs are reported to have used an umbrella made from feathers and gold as a *pantli* – an identifying marker, equivalent to a modern flag – which was carried by their army general.

In the Far East, Greece, India and Babylon, the device also became a symbol of power, initially used by the wealthy to shelter them from the sun. The handles could be as long as 5ft (1.5m), with the approximate weight of the umbrella averaging 4lb 8oz (2kg), which often resulted in servants holding the portable shade over their high-ranking employers. It is even believed that in Rome, affluent women would dye the covers of their parasols to represent their favourite chariot team! The Chinese were renowned for using natural products such as bamboo to create their frames and they are also credited with being the first to coat their paper umbrellas with wax or lacquer to help protect them from the rain.

Popular in Paris from the 1750s, it was not until the 1780s that the umbrella became all the rage in Britain. Wood and whalebone were used for the body of each con-traption and covered with alpaca or oiled canvas. Ebony, horn and ivory were often carved by artisans and used for decorative handles. It was Englishman Jonas Hanway (1712–86) who we can thank for the increased popularity of the umbrella. Bringing the practice home from his travels abroad, he adapted the design to suit the rainy weather back home, changing the face of fashion by reinventing a device that had previously been considered a feminine accessory into an indispensable accessory for the British gentleman.

By 1800, anyone worth their salt owned an umbrella. Pill boxes, compasses, drinking glasses, pencils and even daggers were incorporated into the 'male' versions, which also used precious metals such as sterling silver and gold plate, malacca or tortoiseshell to create ornate handles. Ways of reducing their considerable weight were sought and in 1852 Samuel Fox, industrialist and resident of Sheffield – home to steel manufacture – invented a steel-framed umbrella by experimenting with the stays of women's corsets to eliminate the problem of excessive weight.

It wasn't long before these essential utilitarian and fashion items were given nick-names. Charles Dickens' popular novel *Martin Chuzzlewit* featured a character called Mrs Sairey Gamp who always carried an umbrella, so the word 'gamp' found its way onto Britain's streets. Others preferred the term 'mush', believing the umbrella's design resembled a mushroom ,while most opted for the shortened 'brolly' as a means of description.

Gradually, production costs dropped and inexpensive umbrellas became accessible to all, making the brolly as important to us today as it was to our ancestors in order to help combat the effects of mother nature.

Did You Know?

The first umbrella shop was James Smith and Sons. It opened in 1830 at 53 New Oxford Street, London, where it remains to this day. Could you have inherited one of its early examples?

BUTTONS

The majority of us, we would consider ourselves extremely lucky if any of our ancestors' clothes had survived, as this would enable us to understand more about the fashions they wore and the quality and feel of the fabrics from a particular era. When someone passed away it was natural for the next generation to believe that their predecessor's tastes were a little outdated. So unless an outfit was worn for a special occasion, had particular significance in family life or was simply unusual or decorative in its make up and considered worthy of keeping, we have to resort to museum exhibits as a way of picturing our ancestors in period dress.

Don't be disheartened. Tucked away in a small jar, box or neatly folded envelope you may discover buttons that once adorned your ancestors' outfits.

The Victorians were known for their imaginative way of decorating and creating buttons out of every material from mother of pearl to engraved and gilded showstoppers. While the flat, sew-through buttons were produced in their millions to enable trousers and underwear to be fastened, it was the round-faced, shank-backed variety that enabled the artistic button-makers of the day to show off their talents. Fretwork-style works of art competed for attention alongside exquisitely painted miniatures, with pearl work, gilding and mosaic designs all helping to add that individual touch of elegance to a garment. There were times when the buttons on an outfit were as important as the jewellery worn to accompany it.

Although the majority of these buttons were handmade in order to achieve the attention to detail, by the mid-nineteenth century, machine-made buttons enabled mass-market production. Alongside the simple mother-of-pearl variety were a selection of ceramic styles, and by the 1860s the white china button was introduced.

By examining the buttons and envisioning the type of garment they were originally made for, you can begin to build a picture of the wearer.

Ask yourself:
* How popular would the button have been at a particular time?
* Would it have been cheap or expensive to produce, hand- or machine-made?
* Would the button have added value to the garment, making it more expensive to purchase, or was it simply a practical fastening mechanism?
* Could your ancestor have purchased garments from overseas or expensive British-made clothes that were embellished with fine porcelain buttons decorated with hand-painted designs or transfer prints of scenes or flowers? This type of button was usually made in France in the 1860s and although rare today, examples are highly sought after by collectors.
* Take a look in what you may have thought was a worthless box of buttons and is instead a link to your past and establish whether there are any examples that stand out due to their uniqueness, their decoration or the material from which they were made. You may have heard the phrase 'in my mother's button box' and some of us will remember our own mother sewing, perhaps 'making do and mending'

garments during the war years when clothing was scarce and limited by rationing. Can you picture her, or your grandmother, rummaging through their sewing boxes hunting for replacement buttons, collected over the years and cut from old and discarded clothes for use at a later date?

* Could the buttons have once adorned the clothes of older generations in your family tree?
* Are they individual enough to be able to compare them to garments worn by your forebears in old photographs? Study the images to get an idea of which styles were popular in different periods.

Button Timeline

seventeenth to eighteenth century: Gold and silver buttons, usually made in sets, appeared on the clothes of the wealthier people in society.

Victorian buttons: The most diverse era of manufacture; initially often made in sets. Look out for bone-china examples with a pattern in relief.

late nineteenth and early twentieth century: Parkesine and later Bakelite were popular, hard-wearing and cheap to produce.

art nouveau: Buttons were embellished with organic flowing shapes and decoration.

art deco: Buttons tended to be dominated by geometric designs

Remember

Smaller buttons were not only used on women's clothing, but also on men's waistcoats.

JEWELS, CHARMS AND TRINKETS

Worn since prehistoric times, the pendant was a natural progression from the necklace in the form of a loose, suspended piece of jewellery. Most commonly produced in oval-circular-or heart-shaped designs, these adornments were heavy and quite formal, created from precious metals and enamel often with wirework borders set with exquisite gems and pearls, which were fashionable up to the mid-1800s. During this period and depending on their style, pendants could be worn by both men and women. The latter years of the nineteenth and early part of the twentieth century saw a change in trends to more delicate pieces that reflected and complemented the changing necklines of garments, but by the end of the Edwardian era this type of ornamentation had virtually disappeared.

The locket was another matter. Combining an ornamental front with a hinged compartment that opened to reveal a space inside for storing tiny keepsakes, these pieces of jewellery were often given by loved ones as a token of affection or lasting reminder. The introduction of photography in the 1860s meant that small photographs could be placed inside and carried with the person always. During the Victorian era they were not only gifted at weddings, christenings and on Valentine's Day, but also at funerals, when locks of the deceased's hair could be put inside as a mini memorial. Lockets often had an inset glass panel allowing the contents to be viewed without opening. These are extremely sentimental pieces and are often passed down through the generations within a family.

If you've inherited a locket then the contents would have been deeply important to one or more of your ancestors and a real token of love. The discovery of an example with a small filigree section inside would date it to periods in history when hygiene was somewhat restricted. A tiny cushion or sponge would be inserted on which a few drops of perfume could be added, allowing the wearer to breathe in the pleasant aroma when her companions did not smell quite so sweet.

Not all lockets were purely decorative or sentimental. During the world wars, a selection of British and American military uniform locket buttons were produced that secretly contained compasses in case the wearer ended up in enemy territory and needed help to find his location and plan his escape. This would undoubtedly be a terrific find as they are extremely rare and would also raise myriad questions as to your ancestor's role in wartime, about which you may not have been aware. A whole new line of research could then emerge.

IN MOURNING

Not only did the Victorians enjoy collecting mementoes to celebrate events and occasions in their lives, but, obsessed with the afterlife, they were also diligent about keeping lasting reminders of those who had passed away. To appreciate why these items were so important to them we must first try to understand the Victorian mourning customs and traditions.

The burial of a loved one was a huge event and required specific funeral garb, jewellery and stationery to record their passing. This mourning memorabilia was kept to show that the individual was never forgotten, with items often turning up generations later when the traditions for burial had changed considerably.

The custom of mourning could last for many months. The woman was expected to stay within the confines of the home for a number of weeks after the death of her husband, permitting very few callers. After about a month, mourning cards were sent out to show that she would now be receiving visitors. These mourning cards, along with memorial cards sent out after the funeral 'in memory' of the deceased, were elaborate affairs. Edged in black, they could range from the elegantly engraved to intricately paper-pierced works of art.

It has to be said that the Victorians also had a tendency to be ghoulish and for those that could afford it, post-mortem photographs were taken of the deceased with their loved ones. This practice was extremely common with babies and young children who had died prematurely due to the high mortality rates at that time. In many cases, this image would be the only one that the parents would have of their offspring. They were rarely photographed in their coffin, but instead in a lifelike pose with their parents, sometimes with their cheeks tinted, eyes open or even painted onto their eyelids. Others were laid out as if simply asleep. This practice was looked upon very differently than if it were to be carried out today. Known by the Latin phrase *memento mori*, the translation of this kind of keepsake was designed to 'remember that you are mortal'.

While in mourning, accessorising a garment was frowned upon. Whitby jet jewellery, made from fossilised coal similar to black glass in appearance, became the only ornamentation that women who were in the first stages of mourning were allowed to wear. Later, it was popular to take a lock of the deceased's hair and preserve it in a piece of jewellery or weave it into an intricate design or series of knots as an adornment. Brooches and necklaces provided the most common format of allowing the item to be displayed close to the heart. Have any of these lasting reminders been passed down within your family?

BAGS OF STYLE

Decorative beadwork reached the peak of its popularity during the nineteenth century. The more unusual items often came from the Continent where there was an endless supply of beads manufactured from glass and other materials, which were beautifully coloured yet cheap to produce. In Italy, Venetians created the exquisite multi-coloured round seed bead and tubular-shaped 'bugle' beads; Bohemia (now part of Czechoslovakia) was well known for its high-quality glass work and had a ready supply of material for bead-making from the offcuts of glass.

For centuries, sewing has been an accepted pastime of wealthy women, who would sit for hours producing beautiful works of art through tapestry, embroidery and patchwork. For those from less affluent backgrounds, sewing was more of an essential skill for the women of the house, who would be expected to make, repair and alter clothes and linens to make ends meet and save the expense of buying new garments with their precious family income. No matter where you were on the social scale, the addition of beads to a garment, bag, accessory or item of household furnishing would always be appreciated.

During the Victorian era, beadwork wasn't limited to fashion items and could be seen adorning lampshades, footstools, cushions, trays, tablemats and decorative boxes, but those pieces that have often stood the test of time and are highly collectable today are handbags. Their shape and usage has enabled them to be easily stored and although a few beads may have been lost through the perishing of threads over time, or perhaps metal beads have become rusty if they've come into contact with moisture, the largest problem is often a slightly musty odour that can usually be remedied by repackaging the item.

Today, we find the bigger the bag the better to enable us to throw everything into it from our mobile phones to the kitchen sink, but back in the mid–1800s this was not the case. Styles dictated that women were at their most fashionable in voluminous, dome-shaped crinolines and to have a pocket to carry any personal items would have spoilt the line of the dress and was therefore out of the question. An alternative had to be found, and appeared in the shape of the handbag, designed to be decorative and feminine and to complement the outfit.

Although handbags could be bought commercially, many women chose to use their needlework skills to design their own, copying existing creations, following patterns or conceiving something entirely new. As a result, this may mean that an example handed down through your family could be truly unique.

From drawstring pouches with beaded tassels to small purses with tortoiseshell fastenings and velvet trim, the array of designs was endless. The jewelled surface and flexibility of the material made them highly coveted accessories. Inspired by images from nature, plants and flowers were the most common motifs. Alternatively, intricate romantic or pastoral scenes and even historical landmarks were followed closely by Asian ornamentation and abstract patterns. Such was the love of beaded items that women not only created and carried their bags to formal occasions but also decorated large bags that they could enjoy at home, and which providing somewhere to store their sewing supplies.

By the beginning of the First World War, the trend for beaded bags began to die out as more practical and functional handbags were required and needlework leisure time for women was replaced with more demanding household tasks. Imports from France continued to be available until the early 1940s. Manufactured by professional companies in the textile industry, they monopolised the market with their highly embellished art deco designs sparkling and shimmering with iridescent beads.

The creations from this particular period are often easier to spot and may help you to date your own items. Egyptian motifs, sequins, gold wiring, mesh and fringing may have been added to accompany the beadwork. Stronger, shaped outer casings often formed the basis of the bag to allow internal inner compartments for lipsticks and vanity items while still keeping the current style of a compact bag that could be held via a strap from the wrist or as a clutch under the arm.

How To

Solve Your Dating Dilemmas

If you are fortunate to have inherited one of these bags, enjoy its representation of the past and a long-forgotten, glamorous period of history.

The earliest beaded bags were knitted in a drawstring style and were known as a reticule. They were usually cinched closed using twisted satin cords woven through the eyelets at the top edge.

Between 1820 and 1830, it became stylish to have the opening support of a metal frame, often with the addition of a small carrying chain. These frames could be made from tortoiseshell, silver and even an alloy of copper and zinc made to look like gold, known as pinchbeck.

Bags from the mid-Victorian era are made with very small, fine beads. Prior to this date there have been examples with as many as 1,000 beads per square inch. Bags from the 1800s often had three well-defined horizontal layers, with the largest section in the middle bearing the motif design.

By the early twentieth century, the materials used to make the hinged opening frames and clasps varied considerably: pearls and gemstones were used to embellish them; filigree work made them beautifully ornate; and natural products like amber and ivory shouted glamour and style alongside the expensive-looking ormolu, an alloy of copper and tin used to replicate gold.

Sometimes older beads from the early 1800s have been reused to decorate a bag made in the 1900s, which can make actual dating a little confusing. Take a closer look inside to try and establish a clearer clue to its age.

Did You Know?

During the eighteenth century it is believed that 40 per cent of slaves from West Africa on their way to North America were transported in ships from the port of Liverpool. It is thought that European traders used glass beads as an item of barter in order to purchase future slaves in countries like Senegal, Gambia and Ivory Coast.

PERFUME, PREENED AND PAMPERED

Women love perfume. From the light and flowery to the heavy and musky fragrances, everyone has their favourites. Even though the perfumes of our ancestors may not have stood the test of time and have evaporated into the ether, the bottles in which they were packaged survive, kept to recollect special occasions, presents from loved ones or just as sentimental memories of fragrances no longer in production.

Step Back in Time

Products to enhance the skin have been highly prized in almost every culture. Essences and oils were extracted from herbs, and flowers such as rose, honeysuckle and fig leaves allowing people to create their own 'beauty products', which would soften the feel of the skin and improve the smell of the body. Every part of a plant was experimented with, from the blossoms and fruits to the bark, seeds and leaves, to capture a particular fragrance.

The Egyptians are credited with being the first nation to use these potions in religious and cleansing ceremonies, later developing them to become essential perfumed cosmetics for women. Commerce also played its part when the growing trade routes enabled spices to spread throughout the world and, in turn, ingredients such as ginger, bergamot, myrtle and peppercorns increased the variety of scents that could be made and mixed with the fruity equivalents of clementine, grapefruit and mandarin.

Not only did the Egyptians like to smell and feel beautiful in life, they also believed that by placing fragrant oils in decorative jars and gold-encrusted urns in the tombs of their dead, they could help keep the deceased's skin smooth in the afterlife. Similar perfumes were used in the embalming process and it is said that the products used on Tutankhamun were so strong that a faint trace of fragrant oil could still be detected over 3,300 years after his death.

The Romans were equally partial to their aromatic fragrances, often applying scents up to three times a day. Pet horses and dogs would be perfumed and at great feasts caged birds would be allowed to fly free, dispensing scented aromas from their wings around the room. The 'power of perfume' was greatest when Cleopatra is said to have greeted Mark Antony on a ship with scented sails. Such was the effect of the beautiful aroma that announced her arrival that when they finally met, it was love at first sight.

The word 'perfume' derives from the Latin word *per fume* meaning 'through smoke', as many early perfumes were incense based. King Louis XV of France loved sweet-smelling products, resulting in his chambers becoming known as the 'perfumed court', as scents were sprinkled liberally on clothes, fans and furniture as well as on the skin. The nobility and wealthy classes enjoyed the lingering fragrances that helped mask some of the more unpleasant smells of the day that were often due to the limited use of soap and water.

France continued to set trends and when its Baccarat factory opened in 1765 it produced unusual and ornate glass bottles designed to be not only practical, but decorative too. Previously, small metal containers known as 'vinaigrettes' were used, which held a small scent-soaked sponge that could be refilled through an intricately cut mesh over the top. These containers were extremely elaborate gilded or enamelled works of art.

Britain's early perfumer, William Sparks Thomson, founded the Crown Perfumery in 1872, where his floral fragrances known as Flower Fairies were greatly admired by Queen Victoria, who allowed her crown image to be used as a luxurious addition to his scent bottles.

Remember

The wearing of perfume and cologne was both a male and female activity. Napoleon spent huge amounts on ensuring that violet cologne and jasmine extract were delivered to him each month, and Josephine's preference for musk resulted in the aroma still lingering in her boudoir sixty years after her death. The giving of perfume was also a romantic gesture and bottles kept by your ancestors could have been presented to them by their loved ones – each bottle with its own tender story to tell.

Perfume is an unstable product and is prone to evaporation when brought into contact with the air. Exposure to light can cause colour discoloration so the remnants of perfume that remain may not be how they were originally intended. Clear, heavy, cut or faceted glass bottles became popular when it was realised that they helped to refract the light away from the scent within and deterred spoilage. Check for chips or cracks in the glass and that the stopper is a tight fit to reduce evaporation.

IT'S A MAN'S WORLD

Without doubt, there are a plethora of 'goodies' that our female ancestors could have passed down through the generations that give us direct links to their past, but what are the items that their male counterparts are likely to have treasured?

Time Flies

Perhaps one of the most prized male possessions would have been a pocket watch – an essential gadget for any man about town. Waistcoats were an important part of male apparel and the watch would have been attached to a chain threaded through a buttonhole, allowing the watch to be slipped easily into a small pocket for safekeeping or until required. Known as fob watches, the earliest designs were introduced in the sixteenth century, but were initially large and often inaccurate timekeepers. By the early to mid-1800s, examples with machine-made parts were developed by the Swiss, enabling pocket timepieces to become more affordable to the working classes instead of purely a luxury for the wealthy.

British watch cases were usually made from silver or gold and hallmarked on both the inner and outer casing. Be aware that cheaper versions were produced from rolled gold, comprising a layered sandwich of gold and base metal, and pinchbeck, an alloy of copper and zinc made to look like gold.

There were a number of pocket-watch designs. Don't be fooled into thinking that your watch is missing its case, you could instead be in possession of a hunter watch, which was completely enclosed within a metal case. Often used by Victorian gents when out hunting, the face was covered for protection with part of the dial visible through a small glass window. Numerals were inscribed on the outer case to enable the owner to tell the time without opening it.

Top Tip

Take a closer look at your watch.
- Ensure that the manufacturer's number matches both the number on the case and on the watch itself to confirm that they belong together and have not been mismatched at a later date.
- Do the buttons on the hunter watch work properly, enabling you to open and close it?
- Don't attempt to repair a watch yourself – take it to a reputable expert, but be prepared to pay for replacement parts that may now be hard to find due to the age of the piece.
- Don't use abrasive polishes to clean the metal, invest in a lint-free, soft cloth to buff the case.
- Be aware that before 1850, watch faces had keyholes to allow the owner to wind up the mechanism. Later this method was replaced with an integral winder providing a simple clue that can help you to date pre-mid-nineteenth century pieces.

Top Tip

- White enamel dials with black Roman numerals were fairly common, but those with larger, bolder numerals could have been railway watches, essential for station masters in order to comply with the train timetables. A small clue like the size of letters or numerals could help point you in the direction of the occupation of the owner.
- Examine the dial. If it is unusually clean it may indicate that the dial has been replaced at some stage or simply that it was well cared for.
- Did you know that a small arrow mark printed on the face or inscribed on the back of the watch indicates that it was a government-issue military watch?
- Look both inside and outside the watch and its case. Has it been inscribed? Have you heard of the person mentioned? Dig out your genealogy data and investigate whether this person resides somewhere in the branches of your family tree. Do you know anything about the event that the inscription commemorates? Watches were often given as retirement and long-service gifts, awarded for academic, professional and sporting achievements, or from a loved one on a special occasion or anniversary. Try to discover more from the clues given.
- Watch design changed rapidly between the late nineteenth and early twentieth century, enabling the design itself to give you clues as to the period in which it was made and, in turn, will help you to whittle down ownership. Look out for styles that are reminiscent of a certain era, such as angular art deco designs linked to the 1920s or 30s, or for the maker's name.

Watchwords to Remember

Perhaps you've inherited a family clock rather than a pocket watch. Before you investigate further, acquaint yourself with a few clockmaker's words.

case: The frame – usually made from timber – that houses the moving parts.
dial: The face of the clock, which is decorated with Roman or Arabic numerals.
escapement: Regulates the rate of the clock or watch.
escutcheon: The ornamental plate around a keyhole, handle or knob.
horology: The art or science of timekeeping or making timepieces.
oscillating: The continuous repetition of movements or vibrations.
pendulum: A method of timekeeping using a swinging weight.

GENTLEMEN'S ACCESSORIES

Raiding the male arsenal of accessories can shed light on a masculine world that has long since disappeared. Walking sticks and canes were essential apparel for the Victorian and Edwardian gent, giving the owner an air of importance and style. Depending on the decoration, the cane could also be an expression of wealth and status, with specific canes used for evening and social occasions such as the theatre, and others to accompany day wear for a stroll in the park or to a sporting event.

Ebony and bamboo were the most popular materials used for cane manufacture, but it was the addition of silver fittings and gold-plated tops that would mark them out from their poorer cousins. Engraved inscriptions were often added to those canes presented from one individual to another, providing a way of identifying not only the owner but also the person who presented the gift. Monogrammed initials made them a personalised item.

Alternative designs included those with a novelty value, such as a secret compartment where there might be space for a small drinking flask, cigarette storage or even a small compass hidden in the knob. Horn was used to give a natural look and wood provided the ideal material for carving a variety of differently shaped handles.

Perhaps your ancestor was a little more discreet with his accessorising and enjoyed wearing cufflinks to fasten his shirt cuffs. Perhaps he owned a pair inscribed with his initials entwined with those of the love of his life or a souvenir pair from a special trip abroad. Decorative examples were created for sale on cruise liners as a keepsake of the voyage. The images used included cocktail glasses, dice or depictions of the cruise liner itself. Sporting themes also proved popular and give us clues to our forebears' sporting preferences. Horseshoes, traditionally a lucky emblem, were common symbols used on both cufflinks and tie pins, worn not only by those with a love of horse racing, but also those employed as groomsmen and jockeys.

The example you've discovered may be small in size, but was undoubtedly a decorative essential to your ancestor's wardrobe and is now an irreplaceable keepsake.

FOURTEEN

HABITS AND HOBBIES

What you leave behind is not what is engraved in stone monuments, but what is woven into the lives of others.

Pericles

Progress and development have led to numerous changes in the way we live, our attitudes and our opinions. The items that have been left behind by our forebears relating to the habits and hobbies of their daily lives provide yet more evidence of a constantly evolving world.

THE TOBACCO TRAIL

Today, if we choose to smoke, the risks and hazards to our health are fully understood, but up to the late twentieth century, smoking was often seen as extremely fashionable. Manufacturers strove to find new ways of glamorising tobacco, cigarette and pipe apparel, and you may come across any number of signs among your ancestors' effects that suggest that they enjoyed partaking themselves. Take a look at your family photos and note down the period – especially during the war years – when your forebears are seen with a cigarette between their lips or held discreetly in their hands. Attitudes to this social habit were different back then.

Step Back in Time

The first recorded reference to tobacco was made in 1492 when Christopher Columbus landed in the Americas and encountered what was soon to become a much-loved plant. Despite his initial findings, later discoveries of ancient temple carvings show that tobacco had already been smoked in Central America as far back as 1000 BC. Further afield, the early Mayans had smoked the leaves through pipes made of animal bone and the Aztecs preferred to form the tobacco into crude cigars before smoking, gradually incorporating smoke inhalation routines into their religious rituals. In Britain, tobacco was introduced to the Elizabethan court by confirmed smoker Sir Walter Raleigh.

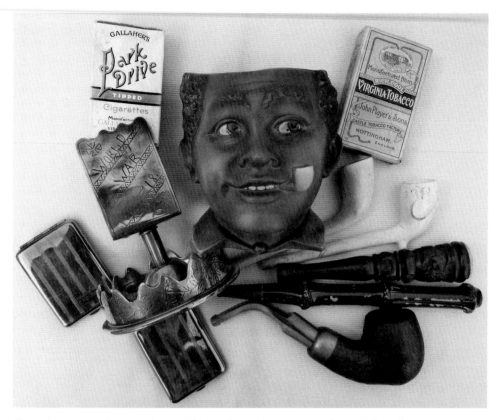

From tobacco pots and pipes to cigarette holders and cases, there are many clues to indicate that our ancestors may have enjoyed smoking. (Stewart Coxon)

As the dried leaves of a plant from the nightshade family, tobacco was originally classified as a drug and could only be purchased from the apothecary. Many practitioners used the leaves as a medical aid, fashioning them into pills, poultices, tinctures and balms, with some believing that once administered, the restorative properties could cure anything from asthma to toothache.

A smokeless, powdered tobacco commonly known as snuff and inhaled through the nose was introduced to the French court during the mid-sixteenth century by Jean Nicot. As a direct result, the tobacco plant *nicotiana* and the active ingredient nicotine were both named in his honour.

Nicotine was extremely addictive, and although reliant upon the import of leaves from Virginia in America, smoking became fashionable in wealthy London society. As a direct result, tobacco became the colony's largest export. Initially, the crop could be sold only to Britain, and the strict trading laws were just one of the factors that helped spark the American War of Independence.

Despite the popularity of the 'lethal weed' there was a staunch band of detractors, principally led by King James I of England, who concluded that tobacco was 'loathsome to the eye, harmful to the brain and dangerous to the lungs'. Later, Russian tsars would ban tobacco use, slitting the noses of first-time offenders as a penalty, and for a time citizens of New France in North America were forbidden to smoke or carry the product on the streets.

As the decades passed, the latest fads saw tobacco used in many forms, from snuff-taking to pipe smoking. Cigars reached Britain after the end of the Napoleonic Wars in 1815 and although cigarettes had been around in a simple form since the 1600s, they did not become all the rage in Europe until after the Crimean War in the mid-1800s when English and French officers returned home with Turkish hand-rolled cigarettes. These cigarettes, although considered slightly effeminate by some, were instantly more appealing, and coupled with the introduction of a cigarette-making machine capable of producing 120,000 cigarettes a day, cigarette smoking became the fashion from the late 1800s.

The cigarette continued its affinity with wartime troops throughout the conflicts of the twentieth century, despite attempts to ban and regulate sales after discoveries about the health risks involved. In the First World War it became an act of patriotism to send tobacco out to the soldiers who were fighting on the front line. Cigarette-smoking heroes returning from the trenches having picked up the habit overseas unintentionally became role models for the cigarette companies. During the Second World War, organisations like the Canadian Red Cross and YMCA would ship tobacco to the forces to aid their relaxation, provide comfort during anxiety and stress and help them through the difficult tasks they had to face. On some occasions, cigarettes were included in rations and companies would send their products for free, ensuring thousands of loyal customers upon their return from conflict due to the addictive nature of the nicotine.

At home, women enjoyed smoking as much as their menfolk, encouraged by the stars of Hollywood movies and advertising glamorising the products. Although we understand the risks today, tobacco usage was viewed in a very different way as recently as thirty years ago.

Pipe Paraphernalia

From primitive clay and Arab crystal pipes to Persian water pipes, a variety of instruments have been created in order to smoke tobacco more successfully. In seventeenth-century England there were two types of clay pipe in use: the popular 'cutty', with a 3in stem often known as the 'nose warmer'; and the 'church warden', with an 8–10in stem, decorated bowl and elegant carrying case.

By the mid-1800s, most well-to-do Victorian gentlemen owned a variety of pipes and smoking accessories. The design of the pipes and the materials used were often a form of status symbol. At this time, a creamy-coloured stone known as meerschaum from the Black Sea region was all the rage. It had good insulating properties and its softness meant it was ideal for carving into a range of decorative designs. The craftsmen would fashion classical and baroque-style heads into the bowls of the pipe, turning their hand from producing the beautiful faces of glamorous women to the grotesque features of gargoyles: whatever your preference there was a pipe for you. To complete the instrument, an amber stem and decorative silver or gold band was added, where you might find the carved initials of the owner or date it was made. The pipe was kept in a made-to-measure silk-or velvet-lined leather case.

If you own a pipe from this period, remember that meerschaum was easily discoloured by tobacco smoke, so don't discount your example as being made from this material just because it is no longer cream coloured. Depending upon usage, meerschaum can range from yellow to nearly black. As a result, some of the carved examples that are of a slightly more grotesque or bizarre subject matter can look better with age. It is the intricacy of the carving and the subject matter that reflect their current value.

Ceramic tobacco pots and glazed jars would have been used to house the loose tobacco. Attractive in their own right, these containers took on a wide variety of designs. Look out for character styled heads with removable hats that would form the pot lid as well as wooden pipe stands used as a resting place for the pipe when not in use.

Smoking Alternatives

When first introduced to Britain, tobacco was expensive, but as it became more accessible it was smoked in a number of forms. The habit brought with it a wide array of accessories indispensable to the fashionable gent and, later, the stylish woman. Pipes, cigarettes, cigars and their associated paraphernalia all had their place, but perhaps you've discovered a small, attractive box in your ancestor's possessions and have now come to realise that they were in fact partial to a little bit of snuff.

What is Snuff?

The habit of taking snuff – powdered tobacco that was sniffed up a nostril rather than smoked – was popular from the mid-seventeenth century onwards, but it was not until the eighteenth century that decorative boxes were used for its storage. Instantly becoming fashionable accessories, these mini cases were even seen as status symbols depending upon the material from which the box was constructed and the type of decoration used.

Made from mother of pearl, tortoiseshell, silver, gold or enamel, the boxes sometimes featured delicate filigree work, fretwork and engraving or were encrusted with precious stones; enamelled scenes depicting a favourite animal, sport or location were often added. These valued items were not limited to the square or rectangular format, but took on many shapes including animal heads and obscure designs.

Don't be fooled into thinking that snuff-taking was restricted to the eighteenth century or earlier. It may have begun to wane in the mid-nineteenth century, but the boxes used were still treasured within a family and were often kept as keepsakes. Your example may have been in the possession of your great-grandfather, but could have been passed down from a previous generation. It is worth turning to your genealogical research documents to locate your family wills and inventories to see if your snuffbox was mentioned in a bequest, which would enable you to link this ornamental token with its original owner.

A ceramic tobacco pot. It was extremely popular to have a tobacco pot in the shape of a head where the character's hat could be lifted to reveal a place for tobacco storage. These would often sit on a mantelpiece as both a decorative and practical piece.

Accessories and Accoutrements

Named after the matches that they held, vesta cases were small storage containers with a rough strip (the striker) along the side that was used to strike the matches on. Made from a wide range of materials including tin, ivory, tortoiseshell, silver and gold, they were beautiful pieces of craftsmanship decorated with enamel, engraving – perhaps even personalised with the initials of the owner – simply embellished with filigree patterns or fashioned into novelty shapes.

Check your own example for signs of wear, chipping to the enamel or gilding, or the possibility of a broken hinge. Unlike American and European examples, most English vesta cases had a small metal ring at the side to enable the wearer to thread the case onto a watch chain.

A selection of Players and Kensitas cigarette cards discovered in an old cigar box. (Stewart Coxon)

Perhaps your ancestor was a cigar smoker. We've all seen the wooden boxes in which cigars are shipped and although they are attractive in their own way, smokers would have preferred a storage method that was a little more decorative. Boxes made of silver, beautifully adorned wood and a variety of other materials not only looked more pleasing, but were lined with cedar to prevent the cigars from drying out. Other examples held a small water container to ensure freshness and were known as humidors.

Although these boxes were extremely attractive, they were more like mini pieces of furniture rather than portable storage devices, so cigar cases were called for, capable of holding three or four cigars that could be slipped inside a pocket. Leather, crocodile skin and silver were popular choices, with some containing a device for extinguishing a half-smoked cigar. If your example looks too small to hold cigars, similar cases were produced to carry cigarettes. Usually in a flat, book-shaped format, they opened up to reveal the cigarettes laid neatly inside.

By the turn of the 1900s, the increased use of cigarettes brought about the introduction of cigarette holders – the more elaborate the better – using attractive materials such as tortoiseshell, jade, silver or the modern plastic, Bakelite. These items were particularly popular with the women of the 1920s who saw the highly embellished holders and decorated cigarette cases as essential accessories to their outfits.

Pocket lighters did not appear until the beginning of the twentieth century and those produced during this period are easily recognisable with their angular lines and art deco style. Lighters were often given as gifts so look out for any personal engraved sentiments, initials or names that could help identify the owner or the date or occasion on which it was given.

Essential Etiquette

We've all seen the films and television programmes that show men socialising together with drinks and tobacco in a relaxing atmosphere of male chat that spans the generations, and it is at this point that the women go off and make their own entertainment. Before they gained their independence and freedom in the twentieth century, women would be expected to withdraw to another room and perhaps sew or read with their female companions.

A STITCHING SALVATION

Throughout the nineteenth century it was assumed that all women from affluent backgrounds would have competent needlework skills. Often in the company of other female family members or friends, the lady of leisure would concentrate her efforts on decorative tapestries, embroideries and lacework, which could be turned into useful household items such as cushions and tray cloths or used to create adornments or motifs for their clothes. They would not be expected to carry out mundane tasks such as mending – this role would be for the seamstress.

Your ancestor may have been a keen lace-maker. Newspaper cuttings and engravings can illustrate how these traditions were passed on and how the lace was fashionably worn during different periods. These examples show 'The Worker' and 'The Wearer', from The Illustrated London News, 29 April 1882.

Needlework is an area where even the smallest item can give us clues to the past. There was a time when almost every woman owned a sewing box and these boxes and their contents are a reminder of the value once placed upon this important household skill.

Most equipment needed to carry out any type of needlework was kept in a portable sewing box, which, depending on the quality, could have been made from walnut, mahogany or rosewood, beautifully inlaid with marquetry or mother of pearl. Once the lid was lifted a removable tray inside allowed the cavity to be sectioned into compartments where needles, threads, scissors, tape measures, pin cushions and thimbles could be stored safely and prevented from rattling around when the box was on the move. These boxes were and still are highly coveted items. The craftsmanship involved in creating the outside decoration was just as important as the expertise needed to fashion intricately carved ivory, mother of pearl or wooden bobbins to hold the skeins of wool, silk and cotton that were wound by hand on to each spool.

Top Tip

Observe the materials used closely. When bone is examined with a magnifying glass, tiny blood vessels should be visible, whereas ivory will have light striations of colour running through it.

Thimbles ranged from simple, mass-produced brass examples to those made of precious metals. Bear in mind that before the 1870s, these objects were believed to be too small to hallmark. Look out for those with unusual motifs or those purchased to commemorate an anniversary or special event. Despite silver being a precious metal, it is very soft, so in the early 1880s Charles Horner invented the Dorcas thimble, which had a strong steel core beneath a silver exterior. If you're unsure whether or not you own one of these revolutionary pieces, test to see if the thimble is attracted to a magnet. Pure-silver thimbles may not be magnetic, but they are usually more valuable in monetary terms.

Some thimbles made of porcelain, silver or gilt were painted or engraved with the owner's initials or name and may help you in your quest to match the piece with its original owner. Similarly, an inlaid plaque on the lid or near the keyhole of the sewing box could reveal who had the pleasure of owning such an essential piece of furniture.

Remember that the materials used can also indicate the period in which your pieces were produced. Ivory and sandalwood from the British Empire were fashioned to create items for the home market. Ivory is banned from use in this way today, so consider its availability during particular time frames to help you to date your example and verify possible ownership.

In many cases the more ornately embellished the box and luxurious the interior, the earlier the piece. Look out for tiny scissors with steel blades and silver or gilt handles – often carved to resemble birds – red velvet-lined interiors with contrasting mother of pearl tools or tortoiseshell boxes covered in filigree metal scrollwork. The box may even hold a trade card that could specify from where it was purchased.

Top Tip These high-end pieces of furniture were treasured by their owners, who whiled away many hours creating beautiful works of art.

The introduction of the sewing machine in the late 1800s brought about the decline of the sewing box. Many of the items within were deemed unnecessary when mass-produced needles and pre-wound bobbins came onto the market. By the 1920s a minimal number of items were all that was required and as a result sewing boxes reduced in size. Small velvet-lined cases that held just the bare essentials became popular during the 1930s.

Tools, Techniques and Textiles

A treasure trove of fabric-based items crafted in a particular style have their own stories to tell. Lace-making, for example, was a highly prized skill, practised by women of all classes, with the techniques and tools used passed down from generation to generation. Despite being a traditional form of needlecraft, it can also be regional in style, with areas of the country becoming known for specific patterns and designs.

Step Back in Time

Across the great divide from domestic servants to regal aristocracy, lace as an embellishment has featured on our clothes throughout the centuries. The demand for decoration provided work for thousands of people all over Britain.

The process of lace-making developed from drawn threadwork and, over time, the patterns became more intricate and the stitches were separated from the backing cloth. During the Renaissance period, lace became an essential adornment for garments and dress wear when the demand changed from heavy unconventional usage to a more delicate finer weave for personal embellishment.

In Britain, lace was initially a fashion statement. Used widely in Catholic and Christian churches for christenings – said to be the most important ceremony in the Christian calendar – parents dressed their babies in the finest lace to show their status. The aristocracy and the upper classes wore lace collars, shawls, handkerchiefs and many other garments enriched with elaborate designs and the royal family endorsed lace-decorated attire throughout history, enjoying lavish ruffs and embroidered trimmings.

Queen Victoria wore a Honiton lace wedding gown and matching veil. The christening gown worn by Queen Elizabeth II was handed down for use by her children and grandchildren. Believed to have been made from Spitalfields silk and trimmed with Honiton lace, the christening gown was originally commissioned by Queen Victoria and over the decades has been worn by more than seventy members of the royal family. The high-waisted silk gown has a ruffled lace overlay. In 2008, it was retired and a replica was made. Did your ancestors have such regal aspirations and pass down similar mementoes within your family?

The first lace-makers from overseas who came to settle in England were the Huguenots, French Protestant refugees who were escaping religious persecution in the sixteenth and seventeenth centuries. Over the decades, more followed, using their skills to establish lace villages in the counties of Bedfordshire, Northamptonshire and Buckinghamshire where flax – essential for the threads used in lace-making – has always been grown. It was at this time that Bucks Point lace was developed and named after the county of Buckinghamshire.

Some villages already had a history of making textiles and had a system of out-workers and merchants in place, which made them suitable locations to develop the lace industry. Operating from the small cottages where they lived, they became known as home-workers, and rural households who were not employed in other countryside occupations were able to earn an income. Outwork was usually seasonal, so every member of the family took advantage of work when it was available. Alongside the women and girls some young boys also learned the trade.

Making lace was a complex job requiring skill and the ability to work methodically. Initially a pattern of the lace was pricked out onto strong card from a master card using pins. Indian ink was then applied to mark out the design; this was then attached to a pillow (stuffed with straw to make it firm) and dotted with pins ready to start work. The pins were different sizes depending on the thickness of the thread used. The thread was the largest outlay in the making and would cost the worker a tenth of the price of her lace. If she used fine linen thread produced on the Continent it would add considerably to the price of the finished piece because of the high import duty, so by the nineteenth century fine cotton thread was introduced.

The cotton thread would be passed through a gas flame to remove loose fibres, earning the name 'gassed thread'. To aid the worker, linen and cotton thread was graded by numbers: the smaller the number the coarser the thread. Gimp thread was the more radiant and thicker yarn.

Bobbins were used by the worker to carry the thread; these were personalised not only with the user's name but often with the area of manufacture. Some bobbins had heavy shanks to give them weight to keep the thread tight, others had slim shanks and were weighted by glass beads. Made from various fruit woods or bone, the bobbins could be decorated or inscribed to commemorate special events. During the nineteenth century the most common bobbins marked public executions and were known by the rather macabre name of 'hanging bobbins'. A story tells of a boy named Jack, a sailor from Lavendon, who had a bobbin made for his mother wherever he went in the world. By receiving these bobbins Jack's mother would know he was still alive; they were named 'Jack Alive' bobbins.

Ask yourself:
* Have you discovered bobbins belonging to your ancestors? These would have been not only 'tools for the task', but also much-loved keepsakes, each one with a particular memory, perhaps decorated to remember the birth of a child or the passing of a family member.

* Do you or your relatives own antique lace-decorated garments? From whom and where do they originate?
* Are there stories in your family of a lace-making past, not only as a hobby but perhaps once as an occupation?
* Did these ancestors live in known lace-making areas?
* Could a long history of lace-making ancestors point to Huguenot origins?

During the Napoleonic wars, foreign imports were not allowed into the country, so this era saw the greatest wealth in trading. In the latter part of the nineteenth century, handmade lace saw a drastic fall in sales with the introduction of machine-made lace. Nottingham became the centre of this evolving industry, closely followed by Leicester and Derby when their buildings were revamped into warehouses and factories. Lace machines were converted from framework knitting machines and water and steam power increased their efficiency and output.

What Next?

The 1841 census shows that 46 per cent of heads of households in Ruddington, Derbyshire were employed in the lace hosiery industry; the number had grown to over 50 per cent by the 1851 census. Many other villages in the lace-making counties relied upon lace for their major income. Carry out a little regional research in the areas where your ancestors lived if you believe they may have been employed in this trade. The following museums and websites provide an insight into life in the lace industry:

Honiton Lace Museum and Shop, Allhallows Museum, High Street, Honiton, Devon EX14 1PG; tel: 01404 44966; email: info@honitonmuseum. co.uk; website: *www.honitonmuseum.co.uk*.

The Cowper and Newton Museum, Orchard Side, Market Place, Olney, Buckinghamshire MK46 4AJ; tel: 01234 711516; email: cnm@mkheritage.co.uk; website: *www.cowperandnewtonmuseum.org.uk*.

Ruddington Framework Knitters' Museum, Preservation Trust, Chapel Street, Ruddington, Nottingham NG11 6HE; *www.rfkm.org*. This museum is a real must for anyone who wants to experience their ancestor's life, living and working in a small cottage industry.

History of Bedfordshire Lace *www.sandbenders.demon.co.uk/bobbinlace/ history.htm*.

Branscombe lace-making: the 1871 census shows that 941 men, women and children lived in the small village of Branscombe, Devon, eighteen of whom had other occupations and the remainder worked in farming or lace-making. Could one of these lace-makers be your ancestor? For more information, visit *www.laceguild.demon.co.uk/craft/branscombe.html*.

English Lace

Handmade laces comprise of tatting, crochet, needlepoint and bobbin lace and could be made by plaiting, looping, knotting or twisting. It became known by the place of manufacture because of the different techniques used in each area to create unusual patterns.

Bucks Point lace: Made on the Bucks Point grid, with holes running in a 60° vertical pattern, often surrounded by a thicker thread called gimp, which emphasised the pattern. Similar to Punta d'Arenys lace made on the Catalan coast of Spain, Bucks Point lace is honeycombed with picot edges.

Downton lace: Made in Wiltshire and comparable to Torchon lace (see European Lace, below).

Honiton lace: A delicate lace from Devon decorated with roses, shamrocks or thistles. Made separately, these motifs are then joined together by brides, plaits and picots.

Midland lace: Made in Bedfordshire, Buckinghamshire, Northamptonshire and Cambridgeshire; sometimes called Maltese lace, with its plaits and picot edges. A piece of Maltese lace embellished with a cross was shown at Crystal Palace's Great Exhibition in 1851 in London and was later copied so that people could afford a cheaper alternative.

European Lace

Brussels: A rich full lace.

Chantilly: Fragile, with elaborate patterns.

Mechlin: A delicate lace, diamond meshed.

Torchon lace: Derives from a French word meaning 'duster, cloth or tea towel'. Made from coarse thread and mainly bought by peasants. Not very elegant, with a geometric design rather than flowers and leaves, it was widely known as 'beggar's lace'.

Valenciennes: Similar to Mechlin, but not as full.

NEEDLEWORK KNOW-HOW

As well as creating something practical, needlework is an artistic expression of the individual. Prior to the latter part of the nineteenth century, there was often no pattern to follow and embroideries, tapestries and samplers were designed purely from each person's imagination. These designs often included elements that were important to the individual's life. Trees and flowers showed a devotion to the garden and surrounding countryside, birds and wildlife mimicked their passion for nature or even their pets, a stylised building represented their home and family along with hearts and sentiments referring to special loved ones and friends. Accomplished needlewomen produced intricate work that resembled real paintings but was created with threads; others crafted simple layouts to capture a record of their childhood schooldays or a memorable event.

In the seventeenth century, the use of silks and satins on which to create these masterpiece meant that this type of needlework was a leisurely pastime available only to the wealthy. By the Victorian era, the social divide was breached when a variety of materials became accessible to the masses. Table linen, coverlets and handkerchiefs were embroidered by the women of the household. Some men were also attracted to these works and if employed as soldiers and sailors would bring back exquisitely embroidered fabrics from their travels abroad, especially from Turkey and the Far East. Do any of your family items look oriental in design? Could your ancestor have brought these exotic keepsakes back from far-flung shores? If so, what was their purpose for travelling so far from home? Is this a line of enquiry that you could follow up?

Scenic Samplers

While some of our forebears left details of their lives in handwritten letters or diaries, there are others who preserved this information in stitches. When trade from Europe and further afield increased, textiles, new stitching techniques and patterns were introduced to Britain. Needlewomen would take note of these designs and capture examples in their own embroideries. As a woman's repertoire grew she might swap the techniques with friends or share the stitch patterns with a daughter, enabling them to incorporate these bands of motifs and shapes into their own work. Created on strips of linen, this type of needlework, which could be easily rolled up and tucked inside a sewing basket, became known as a 'band sampler'. The word 'sampler' is thought to derive from the Latin word *exemplum* meaning 'example'.

Gradually, as pattern knowledge improved, the need for the band samplers as reference works became less important. The preferred size of linen changed to a shorter yet wider 'workspace' where the needlewoman's skills could be showcased when the patterns were integrated into the overall design.

Still known as samplers, they were used not only to help educate young girls with their needlework but on other subjects too. Many were themed, some with flowers, others with maps or biblical scenes or were simply created to commemorate an event such as a royal marriage or coronation, or closer to home, a family occasion. Most featured an alphabet or numerical sequence, and once the basics were understood a piece could be customised with the name of the needleworker, details of their family and maybe even images of their pets, the house and area in which they lived. A variety of silks and gold threads were used, and as well as a demonstration of their abilities, for the younger women the creation of a detailed piece of work was seen as a sign of virtue.

Providing essential clues to the family historian, samplers can reveal fascinating details, such as the school your ancestor attended, or can confirm a woman's maiden name. You may even be fortunate to have been left a sampler that is laid out in the style of a family tree: a fabulous treasure and one of a kind. Look out for other evidence such as emblems like tombstones, urns and weeping willows next to family members' names, or the stitching changing to black thread, indicating that the individual mentioned had passed away at the time the piece was made. Stitched verse may hint at the needlewoman's feelings at the time of creation and the addition of a year, incorporated in the design or in one corner, can identify when your ancestor produced the work and, in turn, determine her age.

There are numerous times in history when women were entirely influenced by the men in their lives, from fathers and brothers to husbands and even their sons. Women young and old used these samplers as a way of capturing their thoughts, preserving their voices and presenting their outlook on the world around them.

Did You Know?

Stumpwork is a technique where layers are built up using button-hole stitch to create a 3D raised effect. Perspective was often ignored in these designs, with various elements, not to scale, placed alongside each other in the composition, a method used regularly in the seventeenth century.

QUILTING AND PATCHWORK

During the eighteenth and nineteenth centuries most families knew of someone who had emigrated overseas. Many chose to seek a better life and new challenges abroad, while others took part in mass migrations to escape poverty, famine and religious persecution.

When Britons chose to put down roots in America they took their talents and customs with them. The women particularly liked to share their needlework skills with others, passing on various practices to local inhabitants and future generations. Quilting and patchwork in America was influenced by British immigrants and gradually an American style developed. The British liked to make their quilts in one large piece, but the Americans started to create theirs from smaller blocks of fabric, stitched together to create a patterned layout. Not only did this mean that any scraps of fabric could be put to good use, but also that the quilt in progress could be worked on at any time in any place, as the materials were easy to transport and store. The patterns gave clues to the life of the owner and took their influence from the early pioneering days, with designs known as Harvest Sun, the Windmill and Turkey Tracks being extremely popular.

Ask yourself:
Are the stories and events from your past woven into the stitches of a piece of needlework? The skills and techniques used may have been long forgotten in your family, so display, preserve or have your ancestral legacies professionally restored. These handcrafted items are unique and took perseverance and passion to create and they are worthy of being treasured.

FIFTEEN

SPORTING MEMORABILIA

Do you know what my favourite part of the game is? The opportunity to play.
Mike Singletary

How many times have we heard stories of an ancestor's sporting prowess or achievements? Those immortal words that you've inherited your great-grandfather's batting ability in cricket, your aunt's tennis backswing or your uncle's famous boxing left hook? Often, we laugh it off and think no more about it, but have you ever thought that there might be more to these winning claims than first meets the eye? Accounts of triumph and victory on the sports field may well have been more than just a passing football knockabout with friends and instead be real successes that deserve a place in your family's hall of fame. What's more, there may even be surviving evidence that can support these tales of glory.

PRIZED POSSESSIONS

The word 'trophy' derives from the French word *trophée*, loosely translated as a prize or spoil of war. In ancient times, these trophies took on many different guises, from captured arms and standards won in battles and great stone plaques as a form of recognition, to simple laurel wreaths and vases given to winners of sporting events. Gradually, chalices were introduced and given to the victor. Usually made of silver, the most common was the 'loving cup', which had a long, tapered body on a pedestal, finished with two or more handles. These were physical evidence that one individual or group of people had successfully conquered all others in a particular contest.

For many of us, the definitive sporting discovery would be a trophy or prize inscribed with the name of our ancestor and the date on which it was won, which would give us an instant history and a fantastic clue to follow and find out more. The decorative appeal of a vintage or antique silver trophy may mean that it spent many years in a cabinet or on the mantelpiece of your ancestor's home before being tucked away on their passing or as home decor fashions changed.

Originally, trophies not only represented the sport, but also gave the silversmith an opportunity to show off his work. Depending on the importance of the event, these craftsmen went to town on creating the ultimate keepsake. From large bowls, platters and urns to lidded vessels, loving cups, tankards and medals, these prizes took on a number of formats, often with elaborately engraved sporting scenes and ornate flourishes and cartouches.

Not all examples may be quite as opulent, but they will have equally as much meaning as their illustrious counterparts. Simple bronze, brass and pewter trophies can still proclaim the sporting abilities of your ancestral heritage, while a sporting figurine on top of a tiered wooden base or plinth with a small plaque can detail past achievements.

Ceramic prizes were another method of recording a sporting success with a description of the event and recipient's name either underneath or, later, painted on top of the glaze. These items are more prone to chips, damage or wear. Remember not to dismiss what looks like an old plate in a box of family treasures: turn it over and you may find a painted inscription on the back.

EXPANDING A SPORTING ARCHIVE

Sports memorabilia refers to items that are directly related to a sporting event, athlete or team. Although this kind of memorabilia can be collected for monetary gain, it can also have great sentimental importance to the owner who may have been a huge fan of a particular personality or have attended a great sporting occasion. For the family historian, the discovery of these types of treasures can shed a new light on an ancestor's likes, dislikes and social activities. The clues may not necessarily lie in the awards received by your forebear, but instead in the ephemera from a specific sport, or outfit, equipment or accessories that were collected by the owner.

Look closely at your ancestor's possessions. Highly sought after are those items that have been used or worn during a match, game or tournament. If you're lucky to have provenance – evidence of the item's origins – then you could be sitting on a desirable piece. Caps, gloves, shirts, bats, balls and flags are just some of the examples that fall into this category.

Cigarette Cards
Originally, small cards were placed inside cigarette packets to reinforce the packaging and protect the contents. Gradually, they were illustrated with advertising and varying designs, topics and educational information so that acquiring a full themed set became extremely desirable. Card-collecting is a hobby that can last a lifetime and is an ideal way of educating yourself on the sport loved by your forebears. For those who enjoy collecting cigarette cards with a sporting theme, the requirements for making a purchase can be very strict. Each card is graded from mint to poor condition and the price reflects the state. There are a number of flaws that can affect their value, from tears,

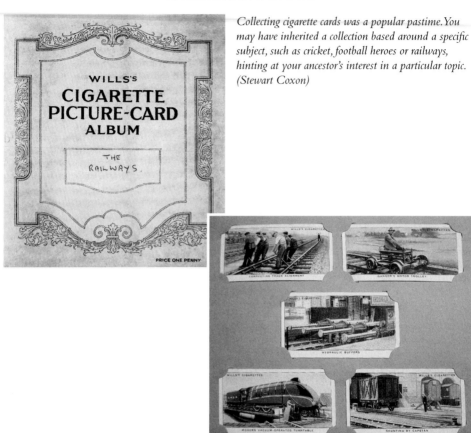

Collecting cigarette cards was a popular pastime. You may have inherited a collection based around a specific subject, such as cricket, football heroes or railways, hinting at your ancestor's interest in a particular topic. (Stewart Coxon)

smudges and deterioration of the cardstock to the printing quality and centring of the image. By grading each of your cards you'll get an accurate idea of how much they are worth: this can be done professionally or you can carry out your own investigations. Special, tamper-proof protective sleeves can be bought to hold your collection, allowing each card to be displayed in its own little pocket.

Sporting Suggestions

If you unearth sports-themed ephemera you may find that this is an area you want to expand upon, collecting more items to enhance your family story and perhaps represent a pastime now played by different rules. Below are a few suggestions to get you started:

* Do your research, not only on your chosen sport, but also on the type of collectables and merchandise you propose to buy.
* There are often copies on the market sold by unscrupulous dealers, so a little background investigation on the item and the dealer could avoid you unwittingly purchasing a fraudulent and ultimately worthless item. It can be difficult to ensure that certain pieces are genuine, especially in an area such as collecting the autographs of players and sporting celebrities: try to get to know their signing habits.

* Always try to establish the track record of the seller before you buy to ensure they are reputable and question the validity of their memorabilia if they are not prepared to offer certificates of authenticity.
* Know from the outset the size of your budget and stick to it. Don't make impulse buys that you could later regret: if a deal sounds too good to be true the chances are it is.
* Get to know other sports collectors and experts via the internet, sports memorabilia message boards or organised collectors' meets. Their knowledge and advice could be invaluable to you.
* Invest in a current price guide to get to know your subject. Good examples can be found on websites like *www.amazon.co.uk*.
* Look out for limited editions or unusual items, but ensure that the piece is accompanied by some kind of provenance.
* Consider how you'd like to display your finds and always think about preserving them to maintain their value for a later date when you may decide to upgrade a piece for a better example, or simply to pass on to other family members.
* Keep an inventory of all your purchases just in case a piece is lost or stolen, and for insurance purposes. You may find that your addiction to the subject results in your purchases becoming serious investments. If this is the case, be aware that the value of collectables can go up as well as down. The popularity and demand for sporting memorabilia often mirrors the current successes of the sport itself, so take this into account if you're seeking to purchase items to add to a collection. Examples that you buy during a sport's black spot may well increase in value when it has a change of fortune.

By expanding on your ancestor's collection you are getting to know more about a sport they loved, may have taken part in and a subject they were passionate about. Names, dates, the census and birth, marriage and death certificates can all provide a fantastic timeline of your forebear's life, but discovering their passions and interests lets you get that little bit closer to the real person.

Step Back in Time

Sometimes known as the 'gentleman's game', cricket has been played internationally since the 1800s, but was first referred to as far back as the sixteenth century, originating in England. Developing in the counties of Kent and Sussex, the first written record appeared in 1598 with the description of a game called 'crekett', derived either from the Dutch word *krick*, meaning stick, or the Old English *cricc*, meaning a staff or crutch. Initially played by children, adults soon began to take an interest in the game, only to be suppressed by the Puritan government and the clergy who objected to the playing of the sport when those involved should have been attending church. With the Restoration of the monarchy during the latter part of the seventeenth century, cricket was looked upon fondly and thought to be a respectable game, becoming a major pastime across the social scale. That said, it was also a major gambling sport, requiring the

Paper ephemera and memorabilia can point to sporting enthusiasts in your family tree.

Gaming Act to be passed in 1664 which limited stakes to £100 – still a huge amount at the time. As a result, and in an attempt to strengthen and secure their bets, some wealthy gamblers became the first patrons of the sport by forming and investing in their own teams. These benefactors, comprising aristocrats and successful businessmen, were also able to influence the press – which was now regularly reporting on fixtures between the early county sides – to promote individual players in their teams.

In 1728, a set of codes of practice were drawn up between the Duke of Richmond and Alan Brodrick, a British peer and cricket patron. These Articles of Agreement ensured a strict set of rules when determining the payment of stake money and distributing of winnings, but it wasn't until 1744 that the Laws of Cricket were established and focused more on the actual sport than the gambling. Drawn up by the gentlemen of the Star and Garter Club in Pall Mall, its members went on to establish the famous Marylebone Cricket Club (MCC) at Lord's Cricket Ground in St John's Wood, London, in 1787, remaining the custodian of the spirit of the sport and providing a periodic revision and upholding of the rules to this day.

Cricketing Correlations
As a result of the popularity of the game, *Wisden Cricketers' Almanack* became the longest-running sports annual in history. John Wisden's cricket career took place between 1845 and 1863, but it was a year later in 1864 when he began to publish his now famed almanac (see Chapter 1). Early *Wisdens* can be hard to find in perfect condition due to worn covers or flaking spines resulting in many having been re-covered.

Top Tip   To identify a rebound copy of **Wisden Cricketers' Almanack**, look at the endpapers. Those in a copy of original condition are packed with advertisements while many re-bound copies are not. Also be aware that the first fifteen editions between 1864 and 1878 have been issued in later years as reprints.

During the First World War, print runs for books were very small, so copies were soon snapped up. The 1916 **Wisden** is very rare, coveted for the 396 obituaries it carried of famous cricketers as well as those unconnected with the sport. Paper shortages during the Second World War also increased demand for the books produced at this time.

For those with even earlier editions, look out for the 1875 paperback which is high on the list of most collector's 'sought after' copies. It was thought that Wisden was about to go bankrupt and only a short print run was produced.

Ask yourself:
* Could your ancestor have been a keen collector of these cricketing encyclopaedias and do you have a rarity nestling in the attic? He may not have been a championship player, but he could well have been an armchair enthusiast.

* Did his passion extend beyond the pages of the books and could there be other items of sporting memorabilia waiting to be found or have any been bequeathed to other members of your family?

Use your previous research experience to investigate the background of other sports in which your forebears may have been interested. Horse racing has often been dubbed the sport of kings, but as we all know, you don't have to be of noble blood to enjoy a little flutter. Football and rugby was eagerly followed by those who enjoyed action on the pitch, while golf attracted avid supporters who watched or tried to imitate every shot by their talented sporting heroes. Programmes, posters, sporting biographies, 'how to' books for those who wished to improve their own game, postcards, prints and written records of specific events can all provide a trail for you to follow.

Remember that clubhouses may have lists of previous members and archives offering information about an individual's involvement. Look out for newspaper clippings reporting sporting successes or incidents. The resources are out there for you to trace your ancestor's sporting connections. It is just a case of finding that initial link and then seeing how far you can take it.

SIXTEEN

KINGS OF THE ROAD

It is better to travel well than to arrive.

Buddha

Where would we be without transport? Our twenty-first-century lives require us to easily commute from A to B, with growing demands to get there more quickly, cheaply and now more fuel efficiently than ever before. Although our ancestors needed the ability to move about, the areas they could cover in a reasonable amount of time were limited. Horse and cart, pony and trap and hansom cabs were all important for carrying both passengers and goods, but the coming of the railways and motorised transport heralded a new dawn.

Public transport provided the means to travel further or on a regular basis, but the invention of the motor car proclaimed independence and the opportunity to explore the world beyond the bus and train routes.

CLASSIC CARS

Henry Ford had a lot to answer for. As inventor of the Model T, his design revolutionised the automobile industry, initiated mass production and helped cement a global interest in motor vehicles that has never waned. From newly awaited specifications to the cult status of certain models, little did he realise the extent to which the world would become obsessed with the car.

Born in Detroit, Michigan, in 1863, Henry Ford developed an interest in engineering from an early age. Although brought up on the family farm, he had no desire to follow in his father's footsteps and instead became an apprentice machinist working and servicing some of the latest portable steam engines. His employment with the Edison Illuminating Company led to a series of experiments and his invention of a self-propelled vehicle, which he named the Ford Quadricycle. Edison was impressed and encouraged the development of further designs.

By 1899, Ford had resigned and ambitiously opened the Detroit Automobile Company, but the vehicles produced were not of the quality that he had first intended, resulting in the business folding after less than two years. Undeterred, Ford gained further backing when he created a 26hp engine and went on to form various alliances as he perfected his designs.

In June 1903, the Ford Motor Company was founded, with investors that included the Dodge brothers, John and Horace. His latest vehicle, named the Ford Model 999 by racing driver Barney Oldfield, went on to set a new land-speed record of 91.3mph, ensuring that the Ford Motor Company became known throughout the United States.

His most successful venture was to create a car that was both affordable and accessible to the average person in the street. With an enclosed engine and transmission, and a steering wheel on the left-hand side, the Model T was introduced to the world on 1 October 1908. In keeping with Ford's desire to keep the vehicle affordable, it went on sale for $825. Every year the price was cut, giving wider access to the American population until it reached an all time low of $360 in 1916.

Cheap to repair and simple to drive, the Model T became the car of choice, and sales continually increased. To meet demand the assembly line was introduced and mass production was achieved: workers could assemble a car in just 93 minutes. Henry Ford took the opportunity to announce that 'the buyer of a Ford car can have any colour he wants so long as it's black': this was partly due to the paint's quicker drying time, but the lack of choice also increased the speed at which the cars could be produced.

It was not only Henry Ford who activated this automobile addiction. In the final years of the nineteenth century, European countries were far ahead of Britain in their horseless carriage vehicle development due to tight laws and restrictions at home. Salvation came on 14 November 1896, when the first London to Brighton run took place to celebrate the abolishment of the Red Flag Act. At last a car could be driven faster than 4mph without a flag man walking in front of the vehicle, paving the way for faster cars to be produced, such as the Rolls-Royce Silver Ghost, which coined the phrase 'the best car in the world'.

In Germany, Karl Benz had built his first car, the Motorwagen, in 1885. At the same time, his contemporaries Gottlieb Daimler and his partner Wilhelm Maybach produced a similar high-speed engine, selling their first vehicle in 1892 under the company name of Daimler Motoren Gesellschaft (DMG).

When Frederick Simms bought the UK patent rights to Daimler's engine in 1893, Daimler became universally known as the first of several companies to produce British-built cars, setting the standards for the various vehicles that followed.

Foresighted Herbert Austin created the three-wheeled Wolseley Autocar Number 1 in 1897, but it had few takers. Undeterred, he built a four-wheeled prototype in 1899 that led to the formation of the Wolseley Tool & Motor Car Company in 1901 and ultimately, the Austin Company four years later.

Between 1930 and 1935 car production in Britain doubled, with over 1.5 million cars on our roads by the end of this period. From the affordable Morris Minors to roadsters like the Humber Ten, the freedom to travel brought with it its own problems and as accidents increased so did the need for the introduction of the Highway Code

(1931) and official driving tests (1934). Speed limits were introduced and by 1935, to aid driving in the dark, cat's eyes were added to the middle of the roads.

TECHNICAL TIMELINE

1880s The first vehicles driven using internal combustion engines were developed by Karl Benz and Gottlieb Daimler in Germany.

1884 Henry Royce established his business and later produced the first motor car with his partner Charles Rolls in 1906: a six-cylinder Silver Ghost.

1889 René Panhard and Émile Levassor set up the world's first car manufacturer, building a vehicle in 1890 with a Daimler engine.

1890 Wilhelm Maybach built the first four-cylinder, four-stroke engine and later went on to create the Mercedes, which shattered the world speed record at the time.

1891 Peugeot car company formed.

1908 Henry Ford's Model T goes into production.

1911 Charles Kettering invented the electric ignition and starter motor while working for Cadillac, seeing an end to the difficult crank process necessary to start a vehicle.

Ask yourself:
* Did your ancestor own a car?
* Are there clues in old photographs as to which model of car they're proudly posing alongside?
* Are any living relatives able to confirm ownership?

Photographs are not the only evidence you can look for to discover more about an individual's love of motoring. Small items like keyrings with a logo key fob could perhaps tell you about the make of car in which they were interested or the automobile club they belonged to. Grille badges issued by motoring organisations like the RAC and AA are another example and were extremely popular with collectors due to their chromed brass and detailed enamelled decoration. Look out for tax discs, petrol coupons and road user guides.

Did You Know?

The Royal Automobile Club (RAC), originally known as the Automobile Club of Great Britain, was set up by Charles Harrington Moore and Richard Simms in 1897. Uniformed patrolmen were introduced in 1904. Three years later it was granted royal approval and adopted its present name. The RAC began the British Grand Prix in 1926 and sponsored the first RAC Rally. Was your ancestor interested in the sporting side of motoring?

The AA (Automobile Association) was established in 1905, with membership growing from an initial 100 to 83,000 by 1914 and shooting up to 725,000 by 1939. Repairers were based throughout the country and this information, along with AA routes and details of AA star-classified hotels, were included in the members' handbooks and guides. Did your ancestor belong to the AA and does their handbook still exist?

What Next?

Today, it is commonplace for most families to own one car if not more, but this was not quite so usual for our ancestors. Even though they may not have been able to afford a vehicle, there was nothing to stop them having a love of all things motoring or aspiring to own one in the future. The discovery of a stash of motoring literature such as car brochures and catalogues could give you a clue as to their favourite make and model; car manuals may point to a passion for the mechanical side while chrome-plated bonnet mascots, car horns, brass lamps and even hand-painted signs and other accessories signal a real enthusiast in your tree.

You may have inherited specific motoring clothing – driving coats, motoring caps, goggles and large gloves were all worn when cars were open to the elements – and these are a sign that the wearer liked to look the part when they were out on the roads.

Consider expanding on their collection by amassing motoring memorabilia from the era in which they were interested, and build a unique picture of what made this particular individual tick. Visit motor museums to expand your own knowledge. Do your research before you buy, be aware of how to spot a fake and consider how much space you have for storage. Start small and stick to a budget and, who knows, you may find the addiction for automobilia is in your blood.

THE MOTORBIKE

Not everyone was enamoured of the motor car and while some people loved four wheels there were those who were attracted to two. The motorbike was a cheaper alternative to the car and although the bike itself could only carry two people there was the option of fitting the rather unwieldy sidecar if more passenger room was needed.

Paper ephemera and advertising may have been kept and leather hoods and hard hats could have been treasured possessions before the introduction of the helmet.

A collection of motorcycle memorabilia.

What Next?

For a hands-on approach, you could visit a related museum to understand more about the vehicles, motorcycles and memorabilia that your ancestor was interested in. There are numerous establishments that have a wealth of information, displays and exhibitions for you to view: one of Britain's best is the National Motoring Museum at Beaulieu in Hampshire, *http://www.beaulieu. co.uk/*. The website *www.classicmotor.co.uk/museums/museums.htm* provides a selection of dedicated museums that have vehicles and road transport on show. Consider carrying out an internet search to find out where examples of specific makes and models are housed. Throughout the summer months vintage car and motorcycle shows and rallies are held up and down the country where you will find examples restored in all their glory. This is a great opportunity to talk to owners and like-minded enthusiasts who will be only too willing to answer your questions and may be able to help date your related photographs and motoring memorabilia.

SEVENTEEN

PLAYTIME AND PASTIMES

Study the past, if you would divine the future.

Confucius

For many of us, our childhood was a happy time with lasting memories of idyllic summers and snow-filled winters where our main objective was to have fun with our friends and family. Life in the past is often viewed through rose-tinted spectacles and was perhaps not so carefree for our parents, who were working hard to provide for us. Similarly, when we look at the stern, non-smiling photos of our forebears – the women in corsetry and restrictive dresses and the men with bushy beards or handlebar moustaches – it is hard to believe that they were ever carefree youths, but in the majority of cases they would have been. Running, shouting and making our own entertainment with the playthings we have is universal and stretches across every generation.

If there is one thing that most people can recollect about their childhood it is their favourite toy, and for our ancestors this would have been no different. The items they would have had as presents would have been a world away from today's electronic gadgets, but loved just as passionately. Toys and games help to shape who we are: our values, knowledge, understanding and education. They enable us to use our imagination, teach us to socially interact with others and in some cases prepare us for our future occupations. When we start our genealogical research we tend to move forward from our ancestor's birth date straight to their schooling, but examining the types of toys they played with may well fill some of the gaps in their childhood lives outside the education system. That battered old box in your grandparents' loft could hold a whole childhood's worth of memories and by examining the materials that each item is made from, and the packaging and theme of the toys you can date each treasure while being transported back to another era.

Step Back in Time

From rocking horses and dolls' houses to spinning tops and building blocks, the great divide of the Victorian classes meant that not all children would receive the latest toys in their Christmas stockings, as the games of the rich differed greatly from those of poorer backgrounds. Factory-made clockwork and mechanical tin toys were highly sought after by wealthy families. Girls were encouraged to play with dolls, dolls' houses, tea sets and kitchen utensils, resembling the daily routine of many women in preparation for their motherly roles in later life, while boys were given toy soldiers, trains and model boats to mimic the occupations of their fathers and get them ready for their future careers.

Those of limited means were not able to provide the same luxuries, but often their children were more inventive as they created makeshift boats from old pieces of wood and wooden dolls from clothes pegs dressed in scraps of fabric. The tradition of hanging a Christmas stocking did not become popular until the latter third of the nineteenth century, but even then, poorer children could only expect to find a few nuts and a piece of fruit and considered themselves to be extremely fortunate if they found a handmade toy inside. Instead, over the festive season, they would make their own entertainment, often singing to the tunes played by another member of the household on their fiddle or pipe. A treat would be the witnessing of a magic-lantern show that could be experienced and enjoyed by all generations of the family. An oil or gas lamp was used to send a beam of light through a glass lens to project images of wild animals or comical scenes onto a screen, creating a sense of wonder and expectation for all.

Although families realised that toys and games were designed to provide entertainment for their children, the continuing developments of the Victorian era also commanded that youngsters should be educated as they played to allow them to develop skills and abilities that would be beneficial to them in adulthood. Jigsaws and pictorial puzzles made children ask questions and the images were themed to teach morality and other virtues. Building blocks encouraged construction challenges and problem solving, and those with the addition of letters or numbers helped children to learn their alphabet and arithmetic. Similarly, push-along toy animals such as dogs or sheep, were designed to help very little children to learn to walk and rocking horses were useful in preparing youngsters for the riding skills needed in later life. For many, rules were strict and Sundays were the exception, when children were expected to play with biblical toys such as a Noah's ark because of its religious connotations.

LOSING YOUR MARBLES

As with all pastimes, the simplest is often the best and the skill involved in playing the game of marbles proved particularly popular. Dating back to cave-dwelling early man, marbles in the form of small pebbles or clay balls were first found in the tombs and pyramids of the ancient Egyptians and on Native American burial grounds. Taking their name from the materials from which they were once made, marbles have also been crafted from metal, glass, ceramics and agates.

During the Victorian era, to increase the desire to win, glass-blown marbles took on a more elaborate appearance. From self-coloured speckled balls to those incorporating a colourful twist, the array of examples was endless and each kind attracted a name,

A wooden solitaire set with a selection of vintage marbles. Have you inherited any toys and games from your ancestor's youth? (Stewart Coxon)

depending on its size and its role within the game. Those in use by the player were called 'shooters' or 'taws' and needed to be between ½in and ¾in in diameter. 'Alley's', short for alabaster, was the term given to the best examples, whereas a 'kimmie' or 'mib' described one of the thirteen marbles placed in a ring at the start of the game.

'Aggie's' were made out of agate or glass; 'bombsies' were used for dropping on the target marble and 'keepsies' – everyone's favourite – were those allowed to be kept by the winner at the end of a game.

Although versions of play varied considerably, the main aim was to flick or roll your marble and to hit your opponents'. To decide who went first, a process called lagging took place where each player tried to get their marble closest to a target line and the winner was allowed the first shot.

Although the first book to include the rules for the game was published in 1815, it wasn't until 1848 that a German glassblower produced a mould for making marbles that he named the Marble Scissors, leading the way for machine production in 1890.

PICK A CARD, ANY CARD

Before the invention of television and games consoles, children would spend their time playing card games with their parents or nannies. Taught from an early age, these were a great way to be entertained, offering lots of social interaction and providing educational qualities and knowledge. Stimulated by the identification of letters, numbers and symbols, children learnt as they played.

Playing cards are thought to have originated in China in the seventh century, but it was not until the 1300s that they were introduced to Europe. At the time they were mostly used for gambling, games of skill and fortune telling. By the eighteenth century, playing cards for children had appeared, illustrated with pictures, educational symbols and, later, were commercially published by companies such as Parker Brothers, A.N. Myers and Co. and De La Rue.

Alongside Happy Families and Old Maid, Snap! became the most popular children's card game and was also one of the easiest to learn and which allowed an unlimited number of players. All fifty-two cards were dealt face down before each player would deal their hand in sequence, watching out for two cards of the same value or colour, such as two twos or two black tens or two similar images. The first player to spot this and shout 'snap!' would take the cards and add them to their hand. The player who accumulated all the cards would be the winner.

A wide variety of companies would use these cards as a form of advertising to promote their own products. Gradually the designs were themed to include children's yard games, circus acts, jungle animals, nursery rhymes or even occupations, opening up the children's world with their images.

POTENTIAL PUPPETEERS

Many of us will have had the pleasure of making our own mini theatres or putting on puppet performances during our childhood and throughout the centuries this has proved to be an enduring form of entertainment.

Puppet theatre and the stories performed on makeshift stages were enjoyed by those as far back as the ancient Greeks. By the Middle Ages, English equivalents travelled the country amusing everyone with mystical plays, but it was not until the introduction of puppets such as Punch and Judy that their popularity really took hold.

Mr Punch was first seen in Britain in 1662 and was recorded by Samuel Pepys after a presentation in Covent Garden by Italian puppeteer Pietro Gimonde. Pepys was so intrigued that he returned to watch the show several times, describing his fascination in his diary. At this time Mr Punch was a marionette and not a glove puppet, but he led the way for future puppetmakers to develop their magical world.

Initially used as a form of entertainment for adults, these iconic puppets were developed into the characters that children still love to this day and were regularly seen performing at Victorian seasides, carnivals and summer fêtes. Independent craftsmen and factory manufacturers soon created smaller versions to be played with in children's homes. Although these products could be bought across the counter, many youngsters had just as much fun making their own versions from wood, paper, scraps of material and any other items they could find.

ADULT ADAPTATIONS

Games that had once been played outdoors were gradually reworked for playing indoors, allowing them to be played on parlour tables. Croquet apparatus was modified with the addition of pockets to create a form of billiards, while smaller adaptations introduced indoor bagatelle, derived from the popular gambling game of the seventeenth century. Its origins (although there are many versions) are said to date back to the reign of French King Louis XIV when his brother Duke Arthur – who himself was a hardened gambler – held a party in the king's honour at his Château de Bagatelle, where a new table game was introduced. Duke Arthur dubbed the game 'Bagatelle'.

The first bagatelles were made of wood and had pins for targets and holes for scoring. The players would shoot balls with a stick or cue from one end of the board and the ball would rebound off the fixed pins into the holes to score points. Although adults played gambling versions in public houses, children also loved the fun part of these action games where they could really get involved, and, along with Tiddly Winks and Shove Half Penny – where coins were 'shoved' using the palm of your hand along a tabletop sectioned off into various score lines – they would entertain themselves for hours.

As the nineteenth century progressed, children began to demand more from their games. Dexterity puzzles required persistence and steady hands to perfect the mechanical games created by manufacturers such as R.J. Journet. Robert Journet opened his toy shop in Paddington, London, in 1878 and gradually began to promote his first dexterity puzzles, known as the RJ Series, from the late 1880s.

In 1893, the Reverend Angelo John Lewis published a book, *Puzzles Old and New*, in which he stated that the dexterity puzzles didn't have a secret or need an intellectual process to solve them but instead relied upon the persistent effort and determination of the operator, referring to the puzzles as the 'motion trick' variety. Each puzzle was usually square, oblong or round in shape and topped with a glass cover. Some required the player to manoeuvre ball bearings or game pieces into the allotted holes and others required the skill to navigate the balancing elements inside.

One of the most famous games was called Pigs in Clover, in which all the balls represented pig figures that had to be transferred into a pen in the centre of a maze, relying on the ability of the player to negotiate the objects within. It was all the rage in 1889 and even appeared in political cartoons of the day. The RJ Journet Series became the world's most popular dexterity glass-topped puzzles, selling millions and entertaining its fans well into the twentieth century. The firm used words such as 'perplexing, pleasing, portable, painstaking and providing profuse pleasure' to describe their games, perhaps even paving the way for today's brainteasers, logic puzzles and electronic games of skill.

Previously, toymakers tended to be talented individuals who worked alone or as part of a workshop team, with each craftsman specialising in a particular technique to create either wooden toys, clockwork items or those with moving parts. By the early twentieth century, the benefits of mass production were realised and companies sprang up across the country manufacturing intricate items. The names of Hornby, Meccano and Dinky became synonymous with quality toy production.

Frank Hornby led the pack in 1901 with his construction kits called Mechanics Made Easy, which allowed children to build their own models from perforated metal strips, nuts, bolts and wheels. These kits were later renamed Meccano, allowing Hornby to set his sights on dominating the model railway market. Tinplate was fashioned into replica cars and other forms of transport, which had wheels that turned and doors that opened, enabling not only Britain but the world to enjoy a tinplate and mechanical revolution.

Enjoyed for both their pleasure and educational purpose, early jigsaws were often cut by hand, their shapes random before the introduction of machine cutting. Although small, these 3½ x 5½in late-Victorian examples would have been quite tricky to complete with no images on the boxes to follow.

Topical events, products and inventions often provided subjects for toys and games. Also used for publicity purposes, this jigsaw puzzle was produced especially for Cunard's White Star Line and is likely to have been sold onboard its ships. Could your ancestor have travelled with this shipping line or might this have been a present brought back from the travels of another family member?

TOOLS FOR THE TASK

When examining your own pieces consider that with each changing fashion the materials used to create these playthings also moved with the times.

From the introduction of naive early clay objects there was a long period where items were generally made from wood and relied upon the manual dexterity, knowledge and skill of the craftsman to construct each design. The launch of metal toys ensured that each piece was robust and allowed a greater range of products to be manufactured, leading to the addition of moving and adjustable parts as well as clockwork mechanisms.

The First and Second World War years saw a shortage of products and the necessity for 'make do and mend' relied upon children making their original toys last and fashioning new items from whatever they could find. Many games produced during the war years were inspired by real events, such as Race to Berlin, Jutland (the original version of Battleships) and Bombarding the Zepps, referring to the German Zeppelin airships. Even the jigsaws used images of important military figures, warships or patriotic flags. These types of games and puzzles are real finds and reminiscent of what the era must have been like for a small boy re-enacting these world events with his pals.

When the Second World War ended, the toy industry flourished with a wealth of new ideas and materials, the most important of which was plastic. Tough and durable, plastic opened up a new style of toymaking and as the cinema began to release the latest cartoon-style films, dolls and action figures were modelled on their onscreen equivalents. Marketing and merchandising began in earnest, creating demand for the products as children collected their favourite characters or items in a set.

In many ways the craftsmanship of the older toys far exceeds that of the items in today's throwaway society. Numerous earlier examples continue to hold their value as collectors and nostalgia lovers aim to be reunited with some of their long-forgotten favourites.

Maybe you've inherited an heirloom from your ancestor's childhood? Consider trying to find out more about this item that plays an important part in your family history.

Ask yourself:
* Is the toy well loved and a little shabby around the edges, indicating that it was played with on a regular basis and was perhaps a particular favourite with the owner, or is it in pristine condition, equally treasured but maybe only played with on special occasions?
* Do the toys fall into a particular theme: educational, religious, female or male based?
* Does one particular toy stand out from the rest? Why?
* Are you able to question relatives to see if they own early childhood toys that have been passed down? Can you create a family collection?

* Consider the type of toys that would have been played with in your grandparents' childhood and compare these with those available in previous generations. Children love to be photographed with their favourite toy: have you any photographic evidence to support this?
* Does this toy still exist somewhere in your family?
* Can you look back though old family diaries where descriptions of childhood toys may well have been mentioned, especially in entries made around the Christmas period? Parents may mention buying their children specific items in their correspondence with other adults. Equally, a child's diary could describe their love of outdoor games such as Hopscotch, skipping to certain rhymes, playing with a whip and top or a hoop and stick or riding their prized bicycle. Indoor activities like knitting, making rag rugs, performing mini theatrical productions or completing a scrapbook could also be mentioned and help you to understand the pastimes that kept your young forebears entertained long before television and computers were commonplace.

DOLL DILEMMAS

The discovery of a doll belonging to one of your forebears is a real treat. You may have previously only ever seen photographs or heard stories about this individual in their adult life and the doll may provide a brief glimpse into their childhood. Its condition can tell you whether the doll was much loved, played with on a daily basis and now a little worse for wear, or if it was equally treasured but kept in pristine condition and only allowed to be played with or handled on special occasions.

Dolls have been used for centuries as both playthings and for depicting religious figures. Early examples have been found in Ancient Roman and Greek graves as well as in Egyptian tombs. Although these primitive models were made from materials such as wood, clay and fur, it wasn't until the sixteenth and seventeenth centuries that dolls were created from wood and wax. 'Bisque', or porcelain-headed, dolls, were popular from the nineteenth century onwards.

Remember

Bisque was a generic term used to categorise both bisque and china dolls. China was a glazed porcelain, while bisque was an unglazed porcelain to which extra colour for the skin tone was added before the second firing to make the face more lifelike.

Check your own example for cracks and wear. Bisque was extremely fragile and prone to damage and breakages, and as a result more durable alternative materials were sought and composition – a mixture of pulped paper, sawdust and glue – helped mass-market doll production to flourish.

Dating your Dolls

When trying to date a doll, look not only at the materials used to create the head, body and limbs but also at its clothing. Clothing styles and accessories on the doll mirror the fashions of the day and could enable you to pinpoint the era in which your example could have been produced. Up until the 1880s, dolls had been dressed as adult females, but from this date onwards the popularity of the French 'Bebe' dolls brought about the trend of clothing them as babies or young children. German manufacturers introduced their own baby dolls in the early 1900s.

Advances in technology in the twentieth century brought plastic dolls to the market that were both hardwearing and less expensive to produce. Styles changed and root hair replaced painted hairlines or little wigs.

Doll Definitions

ball-jointed: Refers to a doll's body that has wooden balls for joints. This type of doll is usually made from composition.

character doll: A term initially used to describe dolls made to look like babies or young infants.

flirting eyes: Eyes that move from side to side.

shoulder head: The head and shoulders are moulded in one piece.

socket head: The head is fixed into an opening in the body of the doll.

stationary eyes: Unblinking eyes that do not move or shut.

weighted eyes: Eyes that have the ability to close due to a small weight in the eye.

BEAR NECESSITIES

Although invented simultaneously in both Germany and the United States, it is the latter that can claim to have given the teddy bear its name. When on a hunting trip in 1902, and with his failure to make a kill, President Theodore 'Teddy' Roosevelt was presented with a captured bear as a target. Totally against shooting a tethered animal, he said 'spare the bear', and when the story and an accompanying cartoon appeared in the *Washington Post*, Brooklyn soft-toy makers took the opportunity to make a stuffed bear and call it 'Teddy's Bear' and the name was immortalised.

In Germany, soft-toy maker Margarete Steiff added a bear to her extensive catalogue and after the Roosevelt incident sold 3,000 to America. Subsequently her bear, with the Steiff trademark button in the left ear, has continued to sell worldwide.

Before the 1920s, bears were modelled to look like real grizzies: a lot more fierce looking than their later cuddly equivalents and created in bear-coloured fur. A decade later and bears appeared in an array of colours, their humped backs softened and their longer arms and snouts gradually shortened. Many still had movable joints, but the original fine wood straw known as excelsior was replaced with kapok and, later, foam rubber.

Between the wars, German company Bing became known for its mechanical bears and Schuco created miniature bears. Despite their huge following, America and Germany did not have the monopoly on production and Britain also caught on to the craze with companies such as Deans, Chad Valley, Merrythought and Pedigree making their own versions.

Top Tip If you know the name of the company that made your bear do a little background research to find out when they were established and the merchandise they created in order to determine the age of your bear.

Be aware that new companies mimic the styles of old bears, so familiarise yourself with the way the original manufacturers produced their bears, what bodily attributes were fashionable during certain eras and the materials used to make them at these times. The difference between plush, mohair and mink bodily coverings can help you to verify the quality. You can then use this information to examine, date and help value your own bear.

Does your bear have a hand-sewn nose or eyes, or was there a special feature like a bow at their neck? Are these still intact? Most bears are well loved and in turn, well handled. Lost ears and furless patches of body may affect their monetary value, but as a family heirloom, the knowledge that the bear was heaped with affection from your forebear is priceless in itself.

To store your bear, wrap it in washed cotton sheeting, which will remove any chemical residue that may react in long-term storage. To enable the fibres to breathe and allow good air circulation, never use plastic packaging. If you wish to use tissue paper, ensure that it is acid-free.

Teddy Terminology
arctophile: A person who loves collecting bears. The term derives from the Greek words *arcto*, meaning bear, and *philos*, meaning lover.
cotter pin: A metal, double-pronged pin used to fasten the disc joints into place, allowing the limbs and head of the bear to rotate.
growler: A voice box located inside the bear that can be activated by shaking.
muzzle: The bear's protruding nose or snout.
plush: This furry fabric has a cut pile on one side creating a soft feel to the bear.

What Next?

You really can't go wrong when trying to discover more about ancestral toys if you pay a visit to one of the country's numerous museums of childhood, where you'll instantly get a feel for the individual items and the materials from which they were made.

Perhaps the most famous is the V&A Museum of Childhood in London's Bethnal Green (see below for address). A visit to its website alone will have you fascinated by the array of information on display, broken down into bite-sized pieces with a history of each item, such as wax dolls, with their unusual features and intricate clothing, and an explanation of the type of characters used on popular card games like Snap! and Happy Families. If your interests have led you out of the Victorian age into a new era then consult the British toy-making section of the museum's website.

At present the museum is working on an exciting project to catalogue, conserve and digitise the archives of four major twentieth-century British toy manufacturers, including Lines Bros, Mettoy, Palitoy and Paul and Marjorie Abbatt. It is eager to hear your memories of a visit to a toy factory or shop, or your experiences relating to the British toy-making industry in general. This could be your opportunity to add your recollections of the past for future generations to enjoy.

V&A Museum of Childhood, Cambridge Heath Road, London E2 9PA; tel: 020 8983 5200; email: moc@vam.ac.uk; website: *www.vam.ac.uk/moc/index.html.* Other childhood museums include:

Highland Museum of Childhood, The Old Station, Strathpeffer, Ross-shire, Scotland IV14 9DH; email: info@highlandmuseumofchildhood.org.uk; website: *www.highlandmuseumofchildhood.org.uk.*

Museum of Childhood, 42 High Street, Royal Mile, Edinburgh EH1 1TG; tel: 0131 529 4142; website: *www.edinburghmuseums.org.uk/Venues/Museum-of-Childhood.*

Sudbury Hall and the National Trust Museum of Childhood, Sudbury, Ashbourne, Derbyshire DE6 5HT; tel: 01283 585305; website: *www.nationaltrust.org.uk/sudburyhall.*

West Wales Museum of Childhood, Pen-ffynnon, Llangeler, Carmarthenshire SA44 5EY; tel: 01559 370428; email: info@toymuseumwales.co.uk; website: *www.toymuseumwales.co.uk.*

A quick internet search should put you in touch with the nearest museum to your area. So why not arrange a visit and find out more about the playthings of the past?

Toy Timeline

Late seventeenth century   Dolls' houses first became popular, initially not as a child's toy but as a pastime for women.

1760   John Spilsbury, an English mapmaker, pastes one of his maps onto a wooden base and cuts it into pieces, creating one of the earliest jigsaw puzzles.

1817   Scottish scientist Sir David Brewster patents the kaleidoscope and sells it as a children's toy. Could your ancestor have been a budding chemist or science buff?

1879   The first Steiff stuffed animals were created by Margarete Steiff. Her design for a bear with movable joints and a trademark button in his ear became the most desirable model of all time and are extremely collectable today.

1902   Toy bears became known as 'Teddy Bears' named in honour of the US President Theodore Roosevelt. The demand for teddies soon swept the world.

1930   Two years after the introduction of Mickey Mouse, Charlotte Clark began making stuffed Mickey dolls and started the Disney merchandising craze.

1935   The board game Monopoly was invented and during its first year on the market became the best-selling game in America.

ONE LAST THING

The books your ancestors read during their early years can tell you a great deal about their likes, dislikes and personalities. Often more likely to have stood the test of time and to have been passed down via the bookshelves of previous generations, action, adventures and classic tales provided an imaginative escape for children. A glimpse inside the covers may give a clue as to whom the book belonged or an inscription may point to your example being given as a Christmas or birthday present during a certain year. School and Sunday-school prizes often took the form of a book to improve reading and education, so look out for a bookplate pasted to the introductory pages that describes this achievement.

From *Wind in the Willows* and *Alice in Wonderland* to *Tom Brown's School Days* and *Huckleberry Finn*, your ancestor's legacy is likely to have provided hours of fun as new and exciting situations were opened up to them. Take a trip into the past and read your newly discovered copy and imagine yourself in their shoes as they were transported into another world.

EIGHTEEN

HOUSEHOLD ESSENTIALS

It is surprising how much of memory is built around things unnoticed at the time.
Barbara Kingsolver

TIME FOR TEA

The beautiful tea or coffee service that once adorned your grandmother's sideboard may now be carefully packed away to protect it from damage or perhaps it is on display in a cabinet. It may have been relegated to the attic and labelled old-fashioned in a world of cafetières and cappuccino makers. It is often hard to imagine what our fore-bears' home lives were really like and many of us will have wondered how their houses were decorated and what kind of appliances they had to make household chores easier. The clues can sometimes be staring us in the face: behind the scenes in a family pho-tograph or tucked at the back of a kitchen cupboard.

The heart of the home is usually the kitchen and that is often the best place to look for inspiration. For the British, many problems were solved and achievements rewarded with a cup of tea in china cups and saucers that may have survived to tell the tale. As some of our staple commodities, we take the drinking of tea and coffee, perhaps sweetened with a spoon or two of sugar, for granted, but for our ancestors this was not always the case.

Step Back in Time

The custom of tea drinking had been commonplace in Asia for centuries, but the habit didn't become popular in England until the mid-1600s after the Europeans had arrived in China and established a series of trade routes between the continents.

Tea was marketed as an exotic medicinal drink available mainly from apothecar-ies and, as such, only the aristocracy could afford the beverage and the serving pieces that accompanied the tea-drinking rituals. Tea parties became popular among the upper classes despite allegations by religious reformers against this dangerous brew and the ruination it would bring on families. When Charles II married the tea-drinking

Catherine Braganza of Portugal in 1662, the culture of tea drinking became so fashionable that alcohol consumption went into decline. Tea importation rose from 40,000lbs in 1699 to over 240,000lbs by 1708 as the craze swept the nation, and gradually tea was being consumed by all levels of society.

Shipments to Britain could take up to twelve months from the Far East. When the East India Company gained the monopoly on the tea trade, it followed its American counterparts by designing clipper ships to replace the heavy English 'tea wagons'. Clippers could sail at speeds of up to 18 knots, helping to reduce the journey time. From Europe, the tea was re-exported to America and the colonies.

Coffee houses across the country flourished with the addition of tea on their menus and some even became known as 'penny universities' as anyone could obtain a pot of tea, conversation and a copy of a newspaper for the price of a penny.

The first official tea shop emerged in 1717 when Tom's Coffee House on the Strand in London changed to a tea establishment called the Golden Lyon, where both men and women were welcome. Tea gardens thrived, allowing drinks to be consumed out of doors accompanied by musical entertainment and concerts. As a direct result, the custom of 'tipping' developed when small boxes were left on each table with the letters T.I.P.S. (To Insure Prompt Service) inscribed on the side.

The Duchess of Bedford (one of Queen Victoria's ladies in waiting) is credited with starting the tradition of taking 'afternoon tea' during the nineteenth century. This consisted of thin sandwiches and small cakes accompanied by a pot of tea, which would revive the flagging feeling she would often experience in the middle of the afternoon. The fashion soon caught on in polite society and maybe even in your household.

Did You Know?

The tea trade had a direct connection to triggering the American Revolution, in which perhaps one of your ancestors or a particular branch of your tree may have been involved. In the American port of Boston in 1773, colonists dressed as Native Americans boarded East India Company ships and unloaded hundreds of chests of tea into the harbour to show their disapproval of a tax on British tea consignments. The incident became known as the Boston Tea Party and throughout the following year other protests, or 'tea parties', took place in Philadelphia, Maine, New York and Maryland.

In retaliation, King George III and a livid British Parliament agreed to the Boston Port Bill, which closed Boston Harbour until the East India Company was reimbursed for its loss of cargo. Despite attempts to end the taxation protests and to quash the smuggling of contraband tea, the incident was one of three major events instrumental in sparking the American Revolution.

Fascinating Facts

To describe the product of 'tea', the Chinese Amoy dialect developed the word *te* (pronounced *tay*) from which our word 'tea' derives. The Chinese Mandarin dialect used the word *cha*, which is where we get the saying 'a cup of cha'. The term 'caddy' derived from the Chinese word used to describe a standard tea-trade container weighing 1lb, while the word 'cash' came from the Portuguese *caixa*, meaning case or money box, and was the currency of tea transactions.

Britain's involvement in the sugar industry dates from the mid-1600s when it took control of Jamaican sugar-cane plantations using slave labour until the 1830s to tend and harvest the cane. This lucrative crop became known as 'white gold' and though it was initially used to sweeten tea it was also gradually incorporated into confectionery. Between the seventeenth and nineteenth centuries it was sold to the public from a large sugar loaf or cone broken off using 'sugar nippers'. After the shortages of the First World War, sugar beet (similar in appearance to a parsnip) became a popular crop in Britain. It provided a healthy income for many of our farming ancestors with all parts of the plant used. Once harvested, the leafy tops would be cut off and used for fertiliser or ploughed back into the soil, while the root was sent to factories and mills to be processed. Could your forebears have had occupational links to this sweet commodity?

There were over 3,000 coffee houses in Britain by 1675. Charles II tried to suppress the establishments, believing they were meeting places where scandal brewed along-side the coffee, but still the public flocked to them. Previously, beer had been the most popular choice of beverage, so with the introduction of coffee, customers were not ejected for drunken behaviour but instead alert and buzzing with new ideas. As centres of political debate and discussion about politics and society, coffee and its accompany-ing coffee houses brought changing times to Britain.

COLLECTABLE CERAMICS

Teapots, cups, saucers, jugs, sugar bowls, tureens and ladles may all have stood the test of time and be a relic of your ancestral past. Ceramic-lidded jars were popular when larders were the only form of cool storage; large pottery chargers, often transfer-printed with blue and white landscape scenes, flowers and decorative foliage, were used to carry the Sunday roast to the table. TV dinners on your lap were unheard of by previous generations and at mealtimes a family would sit down to enjoy their food together; perhaps the only time during their busy lives when they could all catch up with the day's events. These household ceramics are a testament to that time.

Take a closer look at your own examples. The discovery of a manufacturer's name such as Spode, Wedgwood and Minton – popular in the eighteenth, nineteenth and early twentieth centuries – along with an unusual shape or pattern may reveal a hidden gem or rarity. Be aware that brown or mottled stains can be difficult or sometimes impossible to remove and have to be accepted as part of the ageing process. Seek advice on stain removal before taking drastic action like bleaching. These family pieces are part of your heritage so you could display them with pride: plastic plate hangers can be purchased, but avoid those with metal grips that can damage the rims.

WAS YOUR ANCESTOR A ROYALIST?

If you're fortunate to have inherited royal commemorative wares, it could indicate that your ancester was a royalist. Blue and white delftware chargers were produced from the seventeenth century to help with the Restoration of the monarchy, followed by other mugs, plates and tankards embellished with the regal heads of Charles I, Queen Anne and George I.

The coronation of Queen Victoria in 1838 marked the beginning of mass production of this type of celebratory souvenir as items were prepared in advance for sale on and after the event. The young queen's image, bedecked in all her finery, was showcased on jugs and mugs, plates and ornaments, and families who supported the new monarchy treasured any memento. Many people, in true Victorian style, eagerly collected similar pieces produced to mark the various milestones in the queen's life, such as the births of children, jubilee celebrations, and her connections with trade and the British Empire. The items kept by your ancestors point towards their interest in the royal family or their fascination with the size of the empire under British rule. The world was a very different place in the nineteenth century and ceramic ware provides a unique insight into this area of our past caught in the images of a transfer print and decorated with gilding to proudly display on a mantelpiece or in a cabinet.

Worcester, Wedgwood, Copeland and Doulton were just some of the factories that produced these collectables and today the items vary in value depending on the subject matter and condition of the piece. Unusual objects to look out for are those that honour the death of Prince Albert in 1861, which can be difficult to find.

Edward VII's coronation caused a headache for ceramic and souvenir makers when the event was postponed due to his illness from 26 June until 9 August 1902. Factories had already manufactured pieces in advance so those with the latter date can be harder to come by. Was your ancestor fascinated by this change of itinerary or were they more interested in those pieces made to mark the coronation of Edward VIII, which never actually took place, or even his abdication?

Plates and ornaments, jugs and figurines, nothing was safe from some form of majestic embellishment. Was your ancestor a royalist with a small collection of related memorabilia?

Top Tip   Did you know there was a difference between a 'special edition' and a 'limited edition'? A special edition is created for a set time, whereas a limited edition is restricted to a set number of pieces.

COMMEMORATIVE CERAMICS

During the nineteenth century there was a demand for affordable ornaments to mimic the expensive porcelain figurines owned by the wealthier classes. The Staffordshire potteries responded with reasonably priced ornaments that could be displayed on the mantelpiece at the heart of the Victorian home. Since they were intended to stand against a wall, some of these objects had undecorated backs and bases to save on manufacturing costs and these became known as 'flat backs'. Colourful scenes depicted an array of subject matter, including rural and pastoral landscapes and moral and religious themes. The figurines took on the guises of the 'celebrities' identifiable in Victorian life, from military leaders and monarchs to Dick Turpin the highway man.

To identify the character on whom your figurine was based, look closely for telltale signs such as particular props or specific clothing details, which may help with recognition. Consider which ancestor owned the piece to help you whittle down a possible date of production. Burnished gold work was used on pieces between the 1850s and 1870s, but from the 1880s onwards a brighter gold was invented, so try to compare your example with others.

Commemorative ceramics were produced to honour individuals and mark special events. The discovery of such items may point to our ancestors' support of a particular monarch, politician or well-known figure, as well as their desire to celebrate and remember a specific occasion. (Stewart Coxon)

From the simple to the elaborate, victory mugs, plates and other ceramics and memorabilia were produced to mark the end of conflicts. This example celebrates the end of the Second World War. (Stewart Coxon)

These ceramics may be gaudy and not to your taste, but they were extremely popular during the Victorian era and could be found in most homes. The choice of subject matter can also give a hint as to your ancestor's likes and dislikes, for example their love of a particular sportsman, political figure or naval hero.

If royalty didn't interest your ancestor, perhaps you can determine their political persuasion. Along with paper ephemera, newspaper clippings, posters and propaganda, themed ceramics were used to showcase the political opinions, both straight and satirical, of the day. The Victorians continued to use the transfer printing methods perfected in the eighteenth century and developed the techniques to enable mass production to take place. The iconic figures of Disraeli and Gladstone feature on countless wares, but it was Lord Grey's 1832 Reform Act that was the first political act to be recognised officially by the potters. Chartist reforms and memorable strikes were also popular subject matter. Items like these kept by your ancestor not only help us to understand how they liked to decorate their homes, but also their beliefs, passions and morals.

NO PLACE LIKE HOME

You may be surprised by how many household items give us clues to the past, and none more so than the area termed 'kitchenalia'. As the hub of the home, the equipment used in the kitchen is often the creator of memories. Take a closer look in your cupboards, or those of older relatives, and there could well be examples that, although they've managed to disguise themselves as everyday essential gadgets, containers or utensils, are in fact foreigners in a twenty-first-century kitchen. The patterned jug you traditionally use to make custard in at Christmas may well have been part of a larger service once loved by your great-grandmother, the ornate cheese dish may have been the essential storage place before the family bought their first refrigerator, or the old milk churn that now holds a floral feature in your garden could have a story to tell.

Dairy Delights

A trip to the supermarket for our plastic cartons of milk is the norm today and the once familiar sound of the early-morning milk float and the chink of the bottles is now almost a thing of the past. Dairy ingredients were a staple part of our ancestors' diets, but the way in which they were obtained often required much more work than just buying them straight off the shelves.

Even before the advent of specialist machinery and the expanding British dairy trade, most rural families kept a cow, enabling even the poorest households to supplement their diets with milk, butter and cheese. The Enclosure Act of the sixteenth century seized their right to graze on common land, forcing many to buy their products direct from the farmer.

The cows were milked by hand, usually twice a day, by the milker or milkmaid. Sitting on a small three-legged stool, they would place a wooden bucket underneath the cow's udder to the collect the liquid. This was sieved into an earthenware crock pot to allow it to cool. The milker then carried the buckets from the place of milking with the aid of a yoke: a wooden support laid across the shoulders that took the weight of the containers hanging beneath. The stools and naive buckets can be very collectable and are often used as focal points for interior design or as planters. Ask yourself if your items were once used in a more practical way by your forebears. Always remember to check wooden items for woodworm or splits in the grain due to weathering.

Cream of the Crop

Before the milk float, milk was transported from the farms in churns on the back of carts to the surrounding villages or by rail to outlying towns and cities.

During the mid-1860s, many Welsh farmers set up businesses in London. They would keep their cows on the premises in the centre of the city and sell the milk either over the counter of their shops or via milk rounds. Doorstep customers would have their jugs filled by a metal measure straight from the churn. These metal ladles – which came in different sizes – gave out a precise amount and were in use from the nineteenth century up until the Second World War. They can be difficult to find and are often a little rusty, but could they have survived in your family hoard?

Milk churns were filled by the farmer and loaded onto lorries to be delivered to creameries or distribution centres, then cleaned and returned to the farm after use. They were capable of holding 10 gallons and could be made of brass, tinned iron or, later, aluminium. The milk could be cooled by filling the pipes inside with cold water.

In 1880 the Express Dairy Company issued the first British milk bottle. Wiltshire United Dairies (later Unigate) followed suit and delivered the bottles up to four times a day on horse-drawn carts. Although the usual bottle size measured 1 pint, 2-pinters were available and smaller, ⅓-pint bottles were produced for schools. The first bottles had a porcelain stopper held on by wire, but these models were replaced in the 1950s by wide-necked bottles topped with a cardboard disc cap. Often they were decorated with advertising of specific events, such as the Coronation in 1953, or simple emblems of the dairy. Aluminium soon became the material of choice for better hygiene, and tops were created in silver, red, blue or gold to indicate the fat content of the milk.

In order to pay the milkman for their weekly delivery some customers would use tokens instead of money. These were made of metal and could be round, triangular or hexagonal in shape. They were mostly issued by the various co-operative societies, whose details were impressed on the token. Today, the tokens have been replaced by paper vouchers. Metal examples are highly sought after.

What Next?

Maybe you've discovered that an ancestor had a passion for collecting quirky dairy items such as cow-themed designs and wares. The German company Goebel was well known for fashioning novelty items. Staffordshire produced numerous small cattle-shaped jugs known as cow creamers, which are highly collectable in their own right. Imported from Holland in the early eighteenth century, they were first made in Britain in salt-glazed stoneware before experiments in other pottery and porcelain were made, and they became a popular sight in the Victorian kitchen. Why not try to add to an existing collection? To find out more you could visit the Stoke-on-Trent Museums (Bethesda Street, Hanley, Stoke on Trent ST1 3DW; tel: 01782 232323; website: *www.stokemuseums.org.uk*) where a fabulous collection of 667 cow creamers was presented by Gabrielle M. Keiller in 1962 and are now on permanent display.

To discover more about early culinary gadgets and paraphernalia, visit the kitchens of stately homes, where a variety of wares can be seen in their natural, period environment. One of the best examples is Erddig, near Wrexham in North Wales. For details of other National Trust properties near you, visit *www.nationaltrust.org.uk*.

Best Butter and the Big Cheese

Wooden collectables are known collectively as 'treen'. As a material, wood was often used in the kitchen for chopping boards, for the handles of knives and other utensils and also in the production of butter. At the start of the process, milk was poured into shallow pans and left for the cream to rise to the top; it was then skimmed off and placed in a butter churn and agitated until the butter was formed. Glass churns could be used to make small quantities by immersing the internal wooden paddles into the cream then rotating them by turning a handle and gears on the top. Buttermilk could also be removed at this stage before salt was added and the mixture formed into blocks with butter pats.

Butter pats – sometimes known as 'scotch hands' – were wooden paddles with ridged grooves to enable the user to stabilise the butter into 1lb blocks and shape them ready for storage or sale. Sometimes stamps were used to imprint a pattern to identify

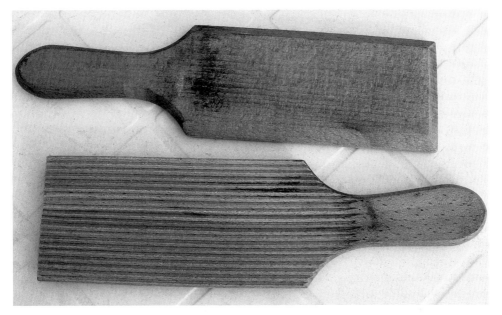

For those ancestors whose life in the country was dominated by agriculture and farming, milking their cattle and producing their own milk, butter and cheese would have been part of their everyday lives. Wooden items like butter pats used to form the butter into solid blocks are examples of family memorabilia that may have survived from our rural heritage.

the maker, with designs that could include thistles, crowns, cows and swans. These stamps were made of sycamore, a wood that did not taint the flavour of the butter. Could buttermaking have been a tradition carried out by your forebears? Even if you haven't come across a set of family butter pats, you can acquire examples at antique fairs on the stalls of specialist treen dealers. Prices are usually very reasonable considering that you are purchasing the tools of a lost art.

The ancient Romans and Greeks considered cheese to be a luxury. The Romans invented a cheese press to improve the curd-draining process, which they later exported to Britain where the technique was perfected further. Even Queen Elizabeth I was instrumental in promoting the qualities of Cheshire cheese in the sixteenth century. But you don't have to have royal blood to enjoy what some people used to call a 'nice bit of mousetrap'. Before refrigeration, cheese was kept on the counter top or in the larder, covered completely with the lid of a cheese dish, which had a small hole in the top to allow it to breathe. These dishes either had a flat rectangular base with a box-shaped cover or a round base with a deep cover, which was ideal for whole Stiltons.

Is there a story behind the large Wedgwood or Doulton cheese dish that now takes pride of place on your dresser? Did it once serve your ancestors as a practical piece of kitchen equipment rather than simply as a decorative ornament?

FURNISHING FUNDAMENTALS

Sometimes it is the most unlikely utilitarian essentials that can give us clues about what life would have been like for our ancestors. Household items are often overlooked when trying to tell this tale. The key is in the word 'essentials'. The legacy of a couple of old candlesticks may have you swiftly repacking them because they don't fit in with your modern decor, but look beyond their style and consider their purpose.

Today we take electric lighting for granted. At the flick of a switch we can light up anything from the garden shed to the Blackpool Illuminations, but for our ancestors the advent of electricity meant that many of the household items they were using became obsolete. Previous generations had used tallow extracted from sheep or cattle suet to create candles and, later, beeswax was found to be a good substitute, burning cleanly without a smoky flame or emitting an acrid odour. Producing these candles was expensive so only the wealthy could afford this luxury while the lower classes continued with their less hygienic tallow equivalent. The growth of the whaling industry in the eighteenth century bought about a huge change in domestic lighting with the introduction of crystallised whale oil known as spermaceti, which was used to form a candle that was hard and surprisingly odour free.

Candle trimmers and snuffers were once part of our everyday household gadgets and are reminders of a time before the advent of electricity when our ancestors' homes were lit with candlelight. (Stewart Coxon)

By the early nineteenth century, the Victorian home was lit with an eerie glow from a mass of candles and oil lamps either suspended from chandeliers, wall-mounted sconces or handheld candelabra and sticks. The style of the period encouraged their decoration with shades or tassels and some devices were mounted in front of mirrors to provide maximum reflection. Ornate and sophisticated oil lamps were covered with glass chimneys to draw the air and prevent the flame from spluttering, resulting in a steady, bright light. With the introduction of paraffin as the new fuel in the mid-1800s, innovative lamp designs were manufactured, allowing more control over the amount of light emitted.

You would be extremely lucky to have inherited any of these early forms of lighting equipment, but if you have, don't limit yourself to the physical objects themselves to tell the story. Search in the background of old family photographs to see if there are any signs of candlesticks on the mantelpieces or paraffin lamps on the windowsills. You can be so fascinated with the human subjects in a photograph that you forget to look beyond them. Remember that many photographs were staged at professional studios during the Victorian era so props were often used that did not belong to the sitter. But ownership of the items is unimportant; the physical evidence of a candlestick explains how their rooms would have been lit, the lack of light produced in the evenings for reading or sewing and the sometimes eerie atmosphere that would have been created.

The introduction of electricity was met with scepticism, but before its arrival, gas installation had generated the same effect. Your ancestor may have been one of the sceptics who was unsure of change. From as early as 1816, gas lighting illuminated many of London's streets and factories, but few used the service in their own homes. Such was the people's distrust of this invisible fuel that it wasn't until the Houses of Parliament installed gas fittings that the population felt safe to use it and recognised its benefits. When gas was used for street lighting, the role of the lamplighter was born – an occupation in which your ancestor could have been employed. Officially providing a service to the community, he would ignite the lamps in the evening and return at dawn to extinguish them. With the aid of a long pole with a small hook at the end, he would light the wicks and replace the oil or gas mantles. His function gradually became obsolete when gas lighting systems were developed that could operate automatically.

Did you know?

In 1879, Thomas Edison and Joseph Wilson Swan both patented the carbon-thread incandescent lamp, refining the ideas of previous inventions and prototypes. The following year Edison created a 16-watt bulb that could last for 1,500 hours.

What Next?

Dig out all those family photographs that have been taken in the home: it is time to take another look at them. Study the image and look beyond the focal point or person in the scene to the clues in the background.

* Perhaps your ancestor is photographed in front of a mantelpiece – what is on the mantelpiece? Are there any framed photographs, decorative vases and ornaments?
* Is there a table in the background? Is it set for tea? Are there any tea-drinking items laid out? Do you recognise the teapot that now sits on a dresser in your grandmother's house?
* Are your ancestors standing in front of a fireplace? Is there a black, cast-iron iron in the grate?
* Are there paintings on the walls of notable figures they admired?
* Can you see the type of switches on the walls? Did they have electric lighting or was there a decorative oil lamp in the window?
* Perhaps your ancestor was photographed outside the house – is there a tin bath hanging on the wall or a mangle in the corner of the yard? These items would provide an insight into their lives without mod-cons.

Once you start asking yourself these questions and looking beyond the main photographic image you'll be surprised what simple facts have been in front of you all the time.

NINETEEN

CHECKLIST

For all genealogists, the universal problem faced by each and every one of us is that once we've found one piece of information about our ancestors we become addicted to finding out more, like a thirst we cannot quench. Although there will be times when some problems seem insurmountable as you face that inevitable brick wall, there will be other occasions when the information you need has been literally staring you in the face from the outset. This book tries to suggest possible alternative resources and ways of prising out information when all other avenues of research seem exhausted.

Perhaps you are sceptical about the amount of information you can glean from your ancestor's possessions and are purely interested in documental resources. If so, you may be missing out on vital clues that could open up a whole new line of enquiry that you had not previously considered or had overlooked. As genealogists we are always taught to revisit our documentation, notes and the records we've collected at a later date to see if there is something we may have missed or if new findings help us to make sense of early problems – so why not do the same with your ancestor's possessions?

TAKE TIME

While some items could reveal more than others, such as the factual details contained in letters and diaries, there are others that can help confirm facts that you already have and strengthen your knowledge. Dates on hand-stitched samplers, details on travel documents or relationships on greetings cards could fall into this category.

Your findings may take you into the realms of another pastime and spark an interest in antiques, collectables and ephemera. These subjects have a dedicated following and many of those involved have no particular interest in the human connection, but instead in the history of the items involved and what they were used for. Could you combine the two areas? Both go hand-in-hand, especially if you want to understand more about life in the past. You may have discovered the 'who' and 'when' and now it is time to reveal the 'what, why and wherefore'. But whatever your ultimate goal, a little extra knowledge can help provide a greater awareness of those ancestors in the attic for both you and future generations to come.

Remember

Now that you've established that there is more than one way to research the lives of your ancestors, use this tried-and-tested formula to get the most from both personal and historical items of importance. Treat each piece individually and thoroughly inspect it.

Ask yourself:
* Who did it belong to? Are you able to date the piece or link it to a specific ancestor?
* Are there any obvious avenues of research that you can pursue?
* What was it used for?
* Why did your ancestor have it in his or her possession?
* Why might they have felt it was important enough to keep?
* Where did it originate from?
* When was it made, produced, created? Is it dated?
* How did your ancestor come by it? Was it a purchase, souvenir, gift from another, award for excellence, a sought-after addition to an existing collection or a utilitarian piece?
* Does it link one or more relatives, like an inscribed love token, a mortgage deed, letter or postcard and, if so, what is their connection?
* Use my companion book *Family History for Beginners* to help point you in the right direction for your research. Understanding the history of an object can help you to fill in the back story and enable you to appreciate why your ancestor owned a particular object in the first place and why they felt compelled to keep it. Depending on the item, individual possessions help us to establish what our ancestors were like simply by examining the physical evidence they left behind. Wills and inventories can also give clues to those special pieces that warranted a bequest to a specific individual.
* Can you deduce whether your ancestor was forward thinking through their love of the latest gadgets and inventions in their lives? Even if they didn't own them, did they keep newspaper cuttings about the latest innovations, showing their interest in technology and science?
* Were they adventurers with a lust for travel to far-off destinations? Did they keep notes and collect ephemera in a dedicated journal?
* Were they unafraid of showing their emotions, perhaps through letters and small, inscribed gifts? Did they have a strong belief in the family unit? Were meaningful items passed down from generation to generation, creating traditions and family customs?
* Did they have a strong work ethic: belonging to trade unions, keeping occupational ephemera, long-service awards or gifts from employers?
* Were they aware of their appearance by purchasing the latest fashions and accessories?
* Can you establish their financial situation: did they seem wealthy or was cash hard to come by?

* Can you determine whether they had an interest in politics, sport or history?
* Does the subject matter enable you to collect similar items to create a homage to this particular area of your forebear's home life, travels or career?

Look beyond the obvious to find the story underneath, such as emotional attachments and the importance of relationships. Think logically about what the item tells you about your ancestor's life and draw up a brainstorming chart to capture your ideas. Once you start you'll realise that there are 1001 questions that you'd like to ask about those who have passed before us. Remember, every clue may be tiny but every clue counts. I hope this book will inspire you to try and find the answers to some of them. Happy hunting and have fun with your latest genealogical quest.

AUCTION TIPS

Have you ever wanted to attend or bid at an auction, but were not sure where to start? Don't be put off by thinking that the larger auction houses, with their impressive sales, are all that are open to you. There are plenty of local auction rooms that feature exciting lots across a wide variety of categories. Your local newspaper will list up-and-coming sales, enabling you to get hold of a catalogue beforehand, which will provide a description of the goods to be sold and a guide price on what each item is expected to fetch. Viewing often takes place a couple of days before the sale, allowing you to inspect the pieces that interest you.

From trinkets and tables to letters and vintage luggage, you are guaranteed to find something new and unusual at each auction you attend. While larger items are sold singly, smaller items may be grouped in lots, so be prepared and set yourself a budget before you attend and *stick to it*! You don't want to overpay, but instead, perhaps pick up a bargain.

Always do your research beforehand. Where possible, visit an auction prior to the sale you are interested in. This will help you to get a feel for the atmosphere and become acquainted with the proceedings. Don't worry about the old tales of bidding on an expensive item that is way out of your league just because you scratched your nose: the auctioneer is experienced and knows how to spot a genuine bid.

Initially, bidding will open at a price started by the auctioneer, but if there is no interest he or she will continue to lower the price until someone takes the bait; the figure will then gradually increase as other bidders join in. Don't get swept up in the excitement and bid more than you intended or on items that you haven't viewed prior to the auction unless you are prepared to take the risk as to the object's condition.

Remember

In addition to the bid price, there is an auction house fee in the form of the buyer's premium. This is usually 10 per cent of your winning bid plus VAT. Each auction house will list its terms and conditions in its catalogue.

If you cannot attend the auction yourself but there is an item that you'd really love to acquire, consider ringing the auctioneer and leaving what is known as a 'commission bid'. On the day of the sale, the auctioneer will try to acquire the item for you as cheaply as possible up to the maximum bid price you had previously stated.

USEFUL WEBSITES

The following websites are some of my favourites for aiding genealogical research, tracking down memorabilia and ephemera as well as increasing my knowledge of life in another era. A simple search of these sites may spark recognition for you and inspire new lines of enquiry.

Ancestry
www.ancestry.co.uk
The world's largest online library of genealogical information.

Findmypast
www.findmypast.co.uk
The most complete online resource of births, marriages and deaths certificates and census returns. New family history records are being added all the time.

The Genealogist
www.thegenealogist.co.uk
One of the leading family history research sites, with a wide variety of databases.

Genes Reunited
www.genesreunited.co.uk
With over 9 million members, this is the place to link up with other like-minded historians and share or swap your findings.

The National Archives
www.nationalarchives.gov.uk
The UK government's official archive, with more than 1,000 years of history waiting to be discovered.

UKBMD
www.ukbmd.org.uk
Essential for finding indexes and transcriptions of births, marriages and deaths certificates as well as census returns, parish records and monumental inscriptions.

Ancestors Onboard

www.ancestorsonboard.com

With over 24 million records of ships sailing to worldwide destinations, use this resource to research those ancestors who have travelled overseas between 1890 and 1960.

Historical Directories

www.historicaldirectories.org

A digital library of local and trade directories for England and Wales, from 1750 to 1919.

British Newspaper Library

http://newspapers.bl.uk/blcs

Holding more than 2 million pages of nineteenth-century newspapers to explore, this is the place to learn more about everyday life and world events at specific points in history.

eBay

www.ebay.co.uk

Perfect for seeking out new additions to your own family archive. Search initially under the 'collectables' category and then whittle down your investigations into the areas that most interest you. Be prepared to spend many hours trawling this ever-changing site.

The Ephemera Society

www.ephemera-society.org.uk

An insight into the world of handwritten and printed memorabilia can help you appreciate the value of the simple items left behind by our ancestors.

Victoria and Albert Museum

www.vam.ac.uk

The perfect place to learn more about everything from fashion to photography, ceramics, paintings and jewellery.

The Imperial War Museum

www.iwm.org.uk

Covering British and Commonwealth involvement in conflicts from the First World War to the present day, the exhibits and information available here can help you to understand more about life during wartime and the experiences of those involved.

National Maritime Museum

www.nmm.ac.uk

Essential for reading up on your naval memorabilia and finding out more about those ancestors with a naval background.

INDEX